2 Chrn 7:14

Lord, HEAL OUR LAND

A Call to Prayer for America

DAVID O. DYKES

Copyright © 2015 N-Courage Resources

For a complete list of books and broadcast messages by Dr. David O. Dykes available in print, CD/Cassette or VHS/DVD, please visit the Discover Life online Resource Center at www.discoverlife.tv. Call toll-free 24 hours a day (888) 539-LIFE (5433).

Green Acres Baptist Church
1607 Troup Highway
Tyler, Texas 75701
www.gabc.org

Produced with the assistance of Fluency Organization, Inc. in Tyler, TX.
Graphic design by DK Designs Group.

To Dr. Jason Holman—the husband of my daughter Jenni, father of three of my grandchildren and my golf buddy.

Also by David O. Dykes

Following Jesus in the Holy Land

Handling Life's Disappointments

The Cloud Strike Prophecy (David Orlo)

HOPE When You Need it Most

Jesus Storyteller: Timeless Truths from His Parables

Angels Really Do Exist: Signs of Heaven on Earth

Revelation: God's Final Word

No, That's NOT in the Bible

Finding Peace in Your Pain

Ten Requirements for America's Survival

Character out of Chaos: Daring to be a Daniel in Today's World

Do Angels Really Exist?

TABLE OF CONTENTS

INTRODUCTION

I BELIEVE WITHOUT A DOUBT THAT AMERICA IS THE BEST PLACE ON THE PLANET TO LIVE. I wrote this book to focus our full attention on our nation—where we started, where we are today and where we seem to be going—and to call us to prayer. In order to understand what has gone wrong in America, we must first remind ourselves of all that is right about our nation. I am passionate about my love for this country, and I wouldn't live anywhere else. Yet I find myself having what some may call a "lover's quarrel" with America because I believe we have moved far away from the godly heritage our Founding Fathers gave us.

Still, I have great hope for our future because our nation has the benefit of sturdy historical, moral and spiritual roots that our forefathers planted long ago within the soil of our national culture. Our foundations are being shaken, as the Bible says, but by God's grace, our roots are still holding strong. If we will turn to God and ask Him to heal our land, I believe with all my heart that America can become a great and God-fearing nation again.

Pastor David O. Dykes

Lord, Heal Our Land

CHAPTER 1

America: A City Set upon a Hill

AMERICA IS UNIQUE AMONG ALL OTHER NATIONS BECAUSE THE PEOPLE WHO SETTLED OUR LAND DID SO BECAUSE THEY WERE SEEKING A PLACE OF RELIGIOUS FREEDOM. In contrast, the French and Spanish originally traveled to the New World looking for conquest, greedily killing thousands of natives for territory and gold. However, the English and other Europeans came to the New World with a new reason in mind. What drove them to endure the harshest seas crossing the Atlantic and the worst winters on the East Coast was the idea of a land of opportunity where they could freely practice their faith.

Although they considered the Church of England corrupt, these Pilgrims weren't trying to get *away* from something as much as they were desperately trying to *find* something new. That something was the freedom to worship the God of the Bible. Our spiritual roots even pre-date our founding as a nation. Did you know that one of the reasons Christopher Columbus wanted to find a new world was so he could take the Gospel there? Even his name means "Christ bearer."

On a chilly day in November of 1620, the Mayflower landed at Plymouth and joined together that same first day to form the Mayflower Compact—the first governing document of Plymouth Colony. Although the original document has long been lost, a copy has been preserved so we can read in their own words why they came to America. The opening remarks of the Mayflower Compact, updated in modern English, mention God four times in just a few sentences (in bold):

> **"In the name of God, Amen.** We, whose names are underwritten, the loyal subjects of our dread Sovereign Lord King James, **by the Grace of God**, of Great Britain, France, and Ireland, King, defender of the Faith, etc.

> "Having undertaken, **for the Glory of God**, and advancements of the Christian faith and honor of our King and Country, a voyage to plant the first colony in the Northern parts of Virginia, do by these presents, solemnly and mutually, **in the presence of God**, and one another, covenant and combine ourselves together into a civil body politic…"

I cannot help but imagine these first settlers recalling these words of Jesus as they thought about their new home, "You are the light of the world. A city on a hill cannot be hidden." (Matthew 5:14) They must have read those words dozens of times back in England, but now they had the rare opportunity to put them into action and build not only a "city" but also a nation that embodied this truth. John Winthrop, a wealthy Christian landowner and preacher who led the second wave of English Puritans to form the Massachusetts Bay Colony, challenged his congregation to realize the magnitude of their responsibility. "We shall be as a city upon a hill," he once wrote in a sermon.[1] "The eyes of all the people are upon us."

Many God-fearing believers came to this land with a strong desire to build a nation that would serve as a witness to the world. The Puritans founded the state of New England. The Quakers founded the state of Pennsylvania. Catholics sought out the area we now call Maryland to try to find peace from persecution. Baptists were also a part of those seeking religious freedom on our shores. In 1638 Roger Williams established the very first Baptist Church in Providence, Rhode Island, so that those who were suffering persecution in Europe could openly practice their faith. Turning closer to home, Williams was also one of the first missionaries to take the Gospel to the Native Americans. As those first decades passed, more and more people seeking freedom and opportunity came to the New World, and they've been coming here ever since.

Some question the founders of our nation

Today many have gone to great lengths to remove any God-talk from the public conversation, throwing into doubt the very reason why our forefathers founded America. Yet they cannot disprove all of the primary sources of history that support the fact that we were founded as a Christian nation. Throughout this book, I cite several examples that clearly show our Founding Fathers' respect for and adherence to the Bible and biblical principles. You may be familiar with some of the quotes and stories—and some may be new to you. However, it's important for us as Americans to read these examples and be more familiar with them so that we can address our Christian heritage without hesitation in a world filled with skeptics.

Our Founding Fathers knew their Bibles. A close examination of documents from men like John Adams and George Washington, including their letters and deliberations, reveals that they quoted the Bible more than any other book. I want to make a case in the next few chapters that what the Bible teaches about the purpose and direction of nations did not escape them and the rest of our forefathers, including: "The Lord foils the plans of the nations; he thwarts the purposes of the peoples. But the plans of the Lord stand firm forever, the purposes of his heart through all generations. **Blessed is the nation whose God is the Lord, the people he chose for his inheritance.**" (Psalm 33:10-12)

Consider the Puritans in New England who formed The New England Confederation as an early type of self-government before the U.S. Constitution was written. Theirs was the first legally binding constitution signed on American soil, and its text began with a firm recognition of Jesus Christ as the Lord in order to provide a clear picture of why they came to America in the first place. The opening remarks reads:

> Whereas *we all came into these parts with one and the same end and aim, namely to advance the kingdom of our lord Jesus Christ*, and to enjoy the liberties of the gospel in purity and peace...

Despite what liberal professors and teachers may try to say about our early history, it is not possible to deny our deep Christian roots without removing or altering many historical texts and sources.

God protected and directed America from the start

Historical revisionists have also tried removing references about how God intervened and protected our forefathers. For instance, from the middle of the 20th century, many U.S. history textbooks omit an amazing episode in the life of George Washington that took place 20 years before the Declaration of Independence. At that time, many of the colonists fought alongside the British during the French and Indian War over disputed territory around present-day Pittsburgh. George Washington was then a colonel fighting for the British under the leadership of General William Braddock.

During the Battle of the Monongahela in 1755, the French and Native Americans easily defeated Braddock's forces because they fired their weapons from safe shelter behind rocks and trees, while the British forces lined up in the open per traditional battle style. Braddock was mortally wounded in the fight, but Colonel Washington continued to rally the troops, despite losing two-thirds of his forces to death or injury. Once he was able to halt the further advance of the enemy, he led the remaining troops to retreat. Due to the heavy fighting, and the shocking death of their general, word soon spread among the troops that Washington had also been killed in battle.

A few days later, Washington wrote a letter to his younger brother John Augustine to report that he was indeed alive. In it he shared the details of how God had miraculously protected him from certain death. In a letter dated July 18, 1755, he wrote: "…by the All-powerful Dispensations of Providence, I have been protected beyond all human probability or expectation; for I had four Bullets through my Coat, and two Horses shot under me; yet escaped unhurt, altho Death was leveling my Companions on every side of me!"

Fifteen years later, Washington was back in the area where he and his troops had endured such heavy fire. An elderly Native American chief who had fought against him in the legendary battle requested to meet "the man who had been protected by the Great Spirit." According to historians, the chief explained to Washington, "You are the man who was divinely protected by God. In that battle I directed my warriors to aim their muskets at you because we knew if we would shoot the leader, the troops would disband. I myself believe I shot you 13 times. And yet you never died."[2]

Schoolchildren enjoyed reading about that miraculous episode for several generations. However, now it has been entirely removed from our history books. Why? Because a public education system based on humanism, instead of biblical principles, has no room for stories about God's divine protection regarding one of His faithful servants. However, their omission does not mean this event—and many others that demonstrate God's intervention—did not happen. American history is replete with examples of God's divine protection of Americans, yet these stories are quickly fading into oblivion.

The Revolutionary War itself is an example of God's protection, considering there were times when Washington's men were barely hanging onto victory by a thread. The British had the strongest, most well equipped army in the world at that time, while the Americans were a bunch of rag-tag, untrained farmers with muskets. Apart from divine intervention and the fervent prayers of many of our leaders and their families, it does not make sense that we would be able to be victorious over the British. You are probably familiar with the American painter Arnold Friberg's painting, "The Prayer at Valley Forge"—a classic among American patriotic works of art. The original work is currently on display at Mount Vernon and shows George Washington kneeling in prayer in the snow at Valley Forge. No doubt, he is praying for God to intervene and protect the men he was leading against a foreign enemy bent on destroying the rebellious patriots—and God answered his prayer.

Although all American children learn that George Washington served as our first president, many are also not told about his first official duty as President. His first act was to pray and ask God's blessing on our nation, according to this excerpt from President Washington's inaugural address on April 30, 1789:

> It would be peculiarly improper to omit in this
> first official Act, my fervent supplications to that
> Almighty Being who rules over the Universe, who

presides in the Councils of Nations, and whose
providential aids can supply every human defect, that
his benediction may consecrate to the liberties and
happiness of the People of the United States...

President Washington's entire speech took less than 15 minutes,
and yet he made reference to God eight times throughout the address.

Men who recognized God's rule designed our government

Our first leaders depended on God and saw America as a testimony
of goodness and righteousness. This is not to say that our forefathers
were perfect. Like us, they were all sinful people who sometimes
struggled to live out their faith. But they all knew the Bible because
it had been their textbook at every level of their education, and they
believed in the power of prayer. When the writers of our Constitution
reached a stalemate in creating the document, Benjamin Franklin
made a motion on June 28, 1787, that he hoped would break the
gridlock. In light of five months of deliberations, he wearily stood
among his peers and explained his rationale this way:

> "I have lived, Sir, a long time, and the longer I
> live, the more convincing proofs I see of this truth that
> God governs in the affairs of men. And if a sparrow
> cannot fall to the ground without his notice, is it
> probable that an empire can rise without his aid?

> "We have been assured, Sir, in the sacred writings,
> that 'except the Lord build the House they labour
> in vain that build it.' I firmly believe this; and I also
> believe that without his concurring aid we shall
> succeed in this political building no better than the
> Builders of Babel.

"I therefore beg leave to move that henceforth prayers imploring the assistance of Heaven, and its blessings on our deliberations, be held in this Assembly every morning before we proceed to business, and that one or more of the Clergy of this City be requested to officiate in that Service."

From that point forward, the group of men asked local Philadelphia pastors to join them in the Assembly Room of the Pennsylvania State House (now known as Independence Hall) and start each session with prayer. Within 10 short weeks, they had completed the Constitution and signed it on September 17, 1787.

With the creation of this document, our forefathers designed a one-of-a-kind form of government unlike anything the world had ever experienced. For example, it created a balance of powers among three branches of government. In reading the *Journal of the Continental Congress*, it becomes clear that they used the Bible and the nature of God as a pattern for the three-fold division of powers. The Bible says, "For the Lord is our Judge (Judicial), our Lawgiver (Legislative), and our King (Executive). It is He who will save us." (Isaiah 33:22)

Another of the most radical aspects of our government's design was the separation of church and state. There had been a close alliance between church and state from the time of the Roman Emperor Constantine, throughout the history of the Holy Roman Empire, all the way to the Church of England. Taxpayers still subsidize the churches in Europe today – whether they attend church or not— amounting to millions of pounds in revenue every year. For instance, the Church of England received the equivalent of about $30 million dollars from the government in 2015, and the year prior the Lutheran Church in Germany received the equivalent of $13 million dollars from the government.

In a grand departure from this historic pattern, our founders decided to do something revolutionary. They loved their churches, but they didn't want to form a state church, collect taxes from the churches or give tax money to the churches. Where did they get this novel idea? We have a specific example of a similar instruction from the Bible that drew a clear line in regards to taxes. Ezra 7:24 states: "You are also to know that you have no authority to impose taxes, tribute or duty on any of the priests, Levites, singers, servants, or other workers at this house of God." Knowing that the men who framed our Constitution had an understanding of biblical principles arms us with the truth when others try to convince us otherwise. Some of these principles are woven into our government's design and are plainly visible if we make an effort to understand the roots of our Christian heritage.

Our first laws guarantee our right to practice and proclaim our faith

In order to appreciate how unique our American form of government really is, we must compare it to other nations. Modern France, for example, has had 15 types of governments in its history, and Italy has endured a staggering 48 different governments. In contrast, our U.S. government has stood strong for the past 24 decades.

I have a trivia question. Is our American government a democracy or a republic? If you remember from your high school civics class, there are basically four kinds of governments. There is a monarchy, which is a rule by one – a king. There is an oligarchy, which is a rule by a few. Next, there is a democracy, which is a rule by the majority of the people. Then there is a republic, which is a rule by law. (Actually, there is also a fifth kind of government, which is anarchy, which is a rule by nobody!) Many Americans mistakenly think we are a democracy because we elect our leaders through a democratic process. However, we are a republic. That's why we say in the Pledge of Allegiance, "I pledge allegiance to the flag *and to the republic* for which it stands…"

Why is it important to understand this distinction? When our Founding Fathers wrote the laws to protect our rights, they ensured that religious freedom was the very first law. In fact, our First Amendment says:

> "Congress shall make no law respecting an establishment of religion, or prohibiting the free exercise thereof; or abridging the freedom of speech, or of the press; or the right of the people peaceably to assemble, and to petition the government for a redress of grievances."

What if a majority of American citizens one day decided that churches shouldn't be tax-exempt anymore? Could they just vote away this privilege? No, our founders established a law protecting that stipulation and designed our government to be a republic so that no one could say, "The majority rules." Instead, when it comes to our rights, we say, "It's the law of the land." We can change laws, of course, but that's a much more difficult process.

However, our religious freedom that is protected by law has been under attack. Let's take prayer as an example. Prayer has always been a part of our public life since our nation was founded; yet the Supreme Court has been systematically dismantling prayer from the public square. They say prayer is fine in the church house, and in a person's home, but it has no place in public education—including graduation ceremonies.

In fact, a few years ago the ACLU sued a high school in Peoria, Illinois, for honoring an 80-year tradition of saying a prayer of blessing at the graduation. Days before the event took place, the Court sided with the ACLU and officially banned prayer at the ceremony. But one of the students giving a speech at the ceremony paused, bowed his head in silent prayer and then he did something extraordinary that turned the ruling on its ear. He faked a sneeze! It soon became obvious that this turn of events was prearranged because after he sneezed, the entire audience and the graduates shouted, "God bless you!"

It was not that long ago that the Supreme Court ruled to affirm that America is a Christian nation. In 1892 they cited and agreed with the ruling of the Supreme Court of New York which stated: "The people of this State, in common with the people of this country, profess the general doctrines of Christianity, as the rule of their faith and practice...**We are a Christian people, and the morality of the country is deeply engrafted upon Christianity.**" You read that right—this ruling originated in New York!

Exactly 70 years later in 1962, our Supreme Court voted 6-1 with two abstentions and ruled that a simple school prayer consisting of 20 words was unconstitutional. Following is the infamous text of the supposedly offensive prayer:

> "To the Almighty God, we acknowledge our
> dependence On Thee. We ask Thy blessings upon us,
> our parents, our teachers and our country. Amen."

In one ruling, 40 million schoolchildren were forbidden to do what everyone in every American classroom had been doing since the founding of our nation. They were suddenly forbidden to start the day just as President George Washington had started his inaugural presidency—by acknowledging and asking for the blessing of God upon America. Next to fall was Bible reading in schools. Soon to follow was legalized abortion and the removal of the Ten Commandments from schools and official statehouses. Today we no longer have absolute standards—which is the definition of moral relativism—and we have become like the generation described in Judges 17:6 where everyone "did what was right in his own eyes." But we've even gone beyond that. We've come to a point where our government is trying to impose their version of morality on the people as the law of the land—hence the ruling by the Supreme Court on marriage in 2015.

Has our nation changed? Absolutely. Has it changed for the better? The facts show the answer to that question. In the two decades of the 1950s and 1960s there were two recorded incidents of violence on a school campus. Compare that to the more than 7 out of 10 students aged 12-18 who said they were threatened or assaulted with a weapon on school premises during the 2014-2015 school year.[3] It seems a school shooting takes place every month these days. We've come a long way in the wrong direction in a short time. America needs to make a U-turn and come back to God.

The light from the city on a hill is fading

President Ronald Reagan also spoke often about America being like a city set upon a hill. In his farewell address to the American people in 1988, Reagan described how he envisioned the country he loved:

> "I've spoken of the city set on a hill all my political life, but I never communicated what I saw when I said it. In my mind it was a tall, proud city built on rocks stronger than the oceans, windswept, God-blessed and teeming with people of all kinds living in harmony and peace. After 200 years, she still stands true on the granite ridge, and her glow has held steady no matter what storm."

I believe that this bright light of moral and spiritual influence is growing weaker. It is our job to fan the flame of freedom before it goes out entirely. Our only hope is not in the one sitting in the White House. Our only hope is in the One who sits enthroned in the heavens. Spiritual warfare is real in America today—if you don't believe it, turn on the news for half an hour. In this next chapter, I want to help us understand the depth of the issues facing us today so that we will know how to pray for our country.

CHAPTER 2

America's Spiritual Heritage–What Happened?

W HICH WORLD LEADER IS DESCRIBED BELOW?

"Times were never better. The national economy was strong during his tenure. Inflation, which had been a plague for two decades, was under control. Peace and prosperity characterized the nation. Many considered him to be one the most gifted politicians to come onto the national stage. One journalist wrote of him, 'Although there was uneasiness over his character and the allegations of corruption and immorality that swirled around him, none of his political opponents could touch him. He was far too slick for their accusations to stick.'

So charming and personable was this leader that even the religious leaders overlooked his lack of integrity. For his birthday, they distributed this prayer to be prayed in the churches all over the country: 'Before you, O Lord, heavenly Father, we remember our leader and President on his birthday. We ask you to continue to help him find the right way in the difficult tasks that yet lay before our nation and to lead all things to a good end.'"

Would you believe these words were published about Adolph Hitler in 1940? In the centuries before Hitler came to power with his maniacal plan to eliminate the Jews and conquer Europe, Germany was one of the most spiritually deep and vibrant nations on earth and the birthplace of Martin Luther and the Protestant Reformation. In a matter of a few hundred years, how could the Germans go from being the seedbed of Christian growth to being a nation that gave us the Holocaust? Could this startling transformation ever happen to America?

It can, if we take our eyes off of God—and it's easier to do than we care to think. In less than 250 years, our nation's spiritual heritage has already flip-flopped from being "one nation under God" to being a nation that does not speak God's name in deference to being politically correct. The Bible has much to say about the blessings bestowed on a nation that chooses to follow and honor Him. However, it also issues warning after warning to those who leave Him out of the equation. "The wicked shall be turned into hell, and all the nations that forget God." (Psalm 9:17)

Our spiritual roots run deep

Sometimes I'll hear someone say, "I'm just lucky to be born in America." I want to reply, "You and I are not lucky to be born here—we're blessed." I heard about a classified in the newspaper that read:

> **LOST:** ONE DOG. BROWN HAIR WITH SEVERAL BALD SPOTS. RIGHT LEG BROKEN FROM BEING RUN OVER BY CAR. REAR LEFT HIP INJURED FROM DOG FIGHT. RIGHT EYE MISSING, LEFT EAR CHEWED OFF. ANSWERS TO THE NAME, "LUCKY."

I'd say that dog earned his name, but we are not merely "lucky" to live in America. If you've traveled much internationally, you know that we are some of the most blessed people on earth to live in a nation where opportunity abounds and we can be free. The reason why we must remember our spiritual heritage and uphold it is because we live in a world that is trying to deny its existence. Sometimes I wonder if our forefathers, in their wisdom, did not anticipate a day like this when some would question whether or not we were founded on godly principles. Maybe that is one reason why they were so bold and unequivocal in their affirmation of our spiritual heritage.

In fact, Senator Daniel Webster (1782-1852) seems to have had a premonition when he wrote only a few years after our founding: "More than all, our government and our country were founded from the very first by faith under the Divine light of the Christian religion. Anyone who would wish that this country's existence had otherwise begun is deceived. Let us not forget the spiritual character of our origin."

It takes some adjusting to get through the 18th century language, but take a moment to read some of the following evidence of our godly heritage:

> **George Washington:** "Did we bring the Bible to these shores? Or did it not rather bring us? The breath of the ancient prophets filled the sails of the tiny ships bringing pioneers to the new world. From these beginnings until now, the Bible has been a teacher to our best men, a rebuker to our worst men and a noble companion of us all."

> **John Quincy Adams:** "The highest glory of the American Revolution was this: It connected in one indissoluble bond the principles of civil government with the principles of Christianity."

> **Connecticut's earliest state constitution:** "The state, the government, owes its origins to the wise disposition of the Divine Providence. The Word of God requires an orderly and decent government established according to God to maintain and preserve the liberty and the purity of the Gospel."

Did you know that at one time in the state of Delaware, every public official (elected and appointed) had to swear to the following oath? Imagine a swearing in ceremony like that taking place today!

> "I do profess faith in God the Father and the Lord Jesus Christ, His one and only son, and in the Holy Ghost, who God has blessed forever more — and I do acknowledge the Holy Scriptures both Old and New Testaments to be given by Divine Inspiration."

Most of us carry an example of our spiritual heritage with us all the time; we just ignore it. The front side of a U.S. dollar bill is fairly self-explanatory. It is the face of our first president, George Washington. However, every part of this currency is a testimony to our belief and our dependence upon God. For example, the eye at the top of the pyramid on the back of the dollar bill was a well-known symbol of God, the all-seeing eye, in Colonial times. It helps to understand that the name for God they often used in the 18th and 19th centuries was Providence. The word "provide" translates from the Latin "pro video," which means *to look ahead, to look over.* That's a good description of God—the One who provides and looks over all. The symbol of the pyramid is also unfinished, something the 18th century statesmen who designed it chose because it showed our country is a work in progress. The two Latin words above the eye, *Annuit Cœptis,* mean, "God has favored our undertaking."

The currency in our pocket says "In God We Trust," signaling that we're depending upon Him for our deliverance. However, even though the dollar doesn't go far today, America is paying a costly price for forgetting the meaning of the symbols on it.

If you look at the signatures of the Declaration of Independence, you'll see another name of one of our Founding Fathers—Benjamin Rush. He wasn't a pastor, but his writings reveal that he spoke like one. His real profession was a physician, but he wrote about his faith with a deep sense of commitment. It is said that Rush was once off-handedly asked, "Are you a democrat or an aristocrat?" I love his response. "Neither," he said. "I am a Christocrat. I believe He, alone, who created and redeemed man is qualified to govern him."

Rush also proposed that the Bible be used as a textbook in every public school and that the government print and distribute a free Bible to every American family. I am a Baby Boomer, which means I am part of tens of millions of Americans alive today who had the opportunity to learn about Bible characters from their public school teachers. My fourth grade teacher was Mrs. Dean, and I always looked forward to her reading us Bible stories after lunch. Likewise, Rush strongly believed that "the universal education of our youth in the principles of Christianity, by means of the Bible" was the best means for sustaining our nation. "For this Divine Book above all others," he wrote in 1789, "favors that equality among mankind and respect for just laws." Rush might be criticized today for taking such a bold stand for biblical truth, but he was respected in his time as the first surgeon general for the Continental Army. He is also called the Father of American Psychiatry, and a Chicago medical school is named after him.

Our values have been reshaped

Those with a liberal agenda often label anyone who opposes their values. Bible-believing Christians who stand up for what they believe the Bible says is right and wrong must prepare to be deemed not only politically incorrect but also something far worse in their eyes: *intolerant.* The time is not far away when I believe Christians will become the target of outright persecution because we're not falling in line with what most other Americans believe about key moral issues.

In the midst of the ongoing cultural revolution, Christians have to be careful about assigning blame for the predicament our nation is in today. We like to point our fingers at others—the Supreme Court, the drug dealers, the abortionists and the pornographers—when *we* have been just as guilty of sin. What sin, you ask? The sin of apathy. We've allowed a lot of these things to happen on our watch. God says in 2 Chronicles 7:14, "If **my** people, who are called by **my** name, will humble themselves and pray and seek my face and turn from their wicked ways, then will I hear from heaven and will forgive their sin and will heal their land." Did you notice God didn't say, "If the abortionists will get right…"? He didn't say, "If the drug dealers get right…" He said, "If *my* people will humble themselves and pray." The responsibility rests squarely on the shoulders of Christians.

When President Abraham Lincoln called for a Day of National Humiliation, Fasting and Prayer in 1863, he made some indicting observations about the state of the nation in a speech he gave on March 30:

> "We have been the recipients of the choicest bounties of heaven; we have grown in numbers, wealth, and power as no other nation has ever grown. *But we have forgotten God.* We have vainly imagined, in the deceitfulness of our hearts, that all these things were produced by some superior wisdom and virtue of our own. Intoxicated with unbroken success we have become too self-sufficient to feel the necessity of redeeming and preserving grace, *too proud to pray to the God that made us.*"

If that was true in the 19th century when Lincoln was president, how much more do we need to issue a nationwide call to prayer and fasting several generations later? We are reaping the consequences of our apathy, hoping that things will "get better" somehow without our having to move out of our comfort zones. Theologian he was not, but Dante observed, "The hottest places in hell are reserved for those who, in times of great moral crisis, maintain their neutrality."

We must renew our commitment to God

It doesn't take a preacher to figure out that we have a choice to make, and we cannot delay our response any longer. General Douglas MacArthur—the five-star general who commanded during World War II and ardent student of history—issued this caution to Americans about the fall-out of immorality in a speech to the Salvation Army in 1951: "History fails to record a single precedent in which nations subject to moral decay have not passed into political and economic decline." America is not the exception to the rule—our downward spiral leads to consequences. MacArthur also learned from history that there are only two choices facing any nation in moral decline. He explained: "There has been either a spiritual awakening to overcome the moral lapse, or a progressive deterioration leading to ultimate national disaster."

What is it going to be? Will we continue to deteriorate as a nation, or will we be part of a spiritual awakening? Before God's people can stand up for His truth, they must first go to their knees in humble prayer and confession. It's time to confess our national sins and repent of the sin of indifference.

I heard about a little girl who was once in New York harbor visiting the Statue of Liberty. The guide explained that the torch symbolizes the light of freedom that America shines to the rest of the world. That night the little girl couldn't sleep, so she went in to her parents' room and said, "I keep thinking about that woman and that torch. I think she needs somebody to help her hold up the light."

She's right—there is a lot of darkness in the world today. However, Jesus said, "You are the light of the world." (Matthew 5:14) There is growing moral decay all around us, yet Jesus also said, "You are the salt of the earth." (5:13) Apathy is a word that was never meant to characterize Christians. The men and women who left their homes in England to establish a new country unlike anything the world had ever seen were a passionate bunch. The rampant complacency about the state of our country among modern Americans—especially Christians—poses a great threat today. As we'll see in the next chapter, God has already given us a sobering example of a nation destroyed by apathy. The similarities between that nation and America, as you will soon see, give strong evidence that we could very well be next.

CHAPTER 3

Will Apathy Destroy America?

PASTOR VANCE HAVNER USED TO SAY THAT PROPHETS, POETS AND PIGS HAVE ONE THING IN COMMON: THEY USUALLY AREN'T APPRECIATED UNTIL AFTER THEY'RE DEAD! Amos, a prophet in the Old Testament book that bears his name, knew something about unpopularity. He had the unfortunate task of telling a prosperous nation the unwelcome news that judgment was coming.

Sensing this would not be an easy job, Amos began his work in the opening chapter by first declaring that God was going to punish the neighboring nations of Damascus, Gaza and Tyre for their sins.

Considering that these were Israel's mortal enemies, I imagine the people probably shouted, "Amen! Preach it, Amos!"

Gaining a little speed, Amos then announced, "And God is going to punish Edom, Ammon and Moab." Once again the people must have roared their approval and shouted, "Amen, brother!" Then Amos went out on a limb and said, "God is also going to punish Judah [the southern kingdom of God's people] for their sins." The Israelites in the northern kingdom didn't like the people in Judah, so that sounded just fine to them.

"Tell it like it is, Amos!" they shouted even louder.

But then Amos added with gravity in his voice, "…and God is going to punish YOU, Israel, for YOUR sins!"

At this, the crowd threw up their hands and laughed at this preposterous idea. Why would God punish a successful nation like them? "You're no prophet," they told Amos. "Go away."

I can relate to Amos. Today if I predicted that God is going to destroy the Middle Eastern nations because they are the hotbed of radical Islam, that message might go over well with many people. Or, if I preached that Russia will disappear as part of God's judgment against atheism, many would say, "Amen!" What if I declared that God is going to bring calamity on Mexico because of the violence and crime from the drug cartels? Some people would heartily support that message. However, despite how unpopular it may be, my message upon the authority of the Word of God has to do with America. Unless Americans repent and turn to God, we are going to face His judgment.

God has a standard for morality

Why was it hard for Israel to believe that judgment was on the horizon? It seemed impossible because God had blessed them so much. Sound familiar? About 40 years earlier at the end of his ministry, Elisha had prophesied a time in the future when Israel would flourish. (2 Kings 13:17–19) Likewise, Jonah had also predicted a time harking back to the opulent days of Solomon. (2 Kings 14:25) And now that prosperous time had arrived and life was good! In fact, the Bible indicates that these people were so wealthy that many had more than one home, both adorned with opulent decorations. God warned, "I will tear down the winter house along with the summer house; the houses adorned with ivory will be destroyed and the mansions will be demolished." (Amos 3:15) It was a time of great prosperity for Israel, but it was also a time of excessive immorality. Instead of humbly thanking God for His blessings on their nation, Israel veered way off track.

God gave Amos a vision of a plumb line to communicate how far they had strayed. Today most carpenters use a level, but for thousands of years builders used this simple tool to inspect their work and ensure a wall was straight. The plumb line uses a long string, and it works on the principle of gravity. Gravity always pulls the line of string straight toward the center of the earth. If someone builds a wall according to that line, it will be straight. However, any builder can tell you what happens if a wall is out of plumb. Even if it's leaning just a little bit, it can lead to all kinds of problems. Amos describes what God told him:

> This is what he showed me: The Lord was standing
> by a wall that had been built true to plumb, with a
> plumb line in his hand. And the LORD asked me,
> "What do you see, Amos?"
>
> "A plumb line," I replied.
>
> Then the Lord said, "Look, I am setting a plumb
> line among my people Israel; I will spare them no
> longer. The high places of Isaac will be destroyed and
> the sanctuaries of Israel will be ruined; with my sword
> I will rise against the house of Jeroboam." Amos 7:7-9

God's plumb line is His Word. It gives us His moral standard for humanity. If someone set God's plumb line against the moral wall America has built over the past 250 years, what do you think it would look like? For much of our history, especially the first 100 years or more, this wall was in line with God's standard. However, in recent decades America began using a different standard to determine right and wrong. God's absolute truth, as contained in the Bible, came into question, and people began going by whatever they felt was right instead. When truth becomes an arbitrary standard, it always leads to disastrous results in the end. America has leaned to the left and right at times, but unless we straighten up and get in line with God's standard, only one thing can happen to a country—it will fall.

It's no surprise then that the idea of God judging America for her sins does not go over well in our modern, self-reliant culture of success. The Israelites did not react well to the prophet's message either. When they told him to stop preaching bad news, Amos essentially told them, "Hey! I am only telling you what God told me to tell you." The Bible records his response this way:

> "I was neither a prophet nor a prophet's son, but I was a shepherd, and I also took care of sycamore-fig trees. But the LORD took me from tending the flock and said to me, 'Go, prophesy to my people Israel.' Now then, hear the word of the LORD.
>
> You say, 'Do not prophesy against Israel, and stop preaching against the house of Isaac.'
>
> Therefore this is what the LORD says: 'Your wife will become a prostitute in the city, and your sons and daughters will fall by the sword. Your land will be measured and divided up, and you yourself will die in a pagan country. And Israel will certainly go into exile, away from their native land.'" Amos 7:14-17

God doesn't play favorites. Israel mistakenly thought she had earned favored-nation status with God. They wanted special treatment, despite their unholy behavior. However, Amos said otherwise. He said, "Hear this word the Lord has spoken against you, O people of Israel—against the whole family I brought up out of Egypt: 'You only have I chosen of all the families of the earth; therefore I will punish you for all your sins.'" (Amos 3:1-2) They were certainly a "chosen" people—chosen to be first in line to receive discipline! Likewise, we should avoid the temptation to think that God will give our country a break when it comes to our disregard for His moral standard.

The same is true on a personal level. God is no respecter of persons. He doesn't deal with you on the basis of your nationality, your race or your bank account. As the Declaration of Independence correctly notes, God has created all people equally. He holds each person accountable for his or her actions. At the same time, no one is too far from the grace of God to find forgiveness and pardon. Since God deals with everyone on the same basis, He's not cutting any special deals for America or Americans. Sadly, the majority of Americans are much more interested in making money and experiencing pleasure than they are in following God's standard, just as they were in the time of Amos.

God despises empty worship

Another reason why the Israelites thought they should be off the hook is that they considered themselves extremely religious. They held religious ceremonies, but their worship was no longer sincere and God knew it. You may be surprised at the harsh words he had to say about their facade of religiosity:

> I hate, I despise your religious feasts; I cannot stand your assemblies...Away with the noise of your songs! I will not listen to the music of your harps.

But let justice roll on like a river, righteousness like a
never-failing stream! Amos 5:21-24

You probably didn't think God could hate anything, but He hates religious hypocrisy. Do you ever show up for church, sing the songs, stand up and sit down and drop a dollar in the offering—while the whole time your heart and mind have been on something else other than your Creator? That's the definition of empty worship. Have you ever gone through the motions on Sunday and lived as you pleased the other six days of the week? That's religious hypocrisy.

America has far and away the most Christians than any other nation on earth. Although the numbers are declining slightly according to recent polls, the large majority of Americans (about 7 out of 10) continue to identify with some branch of the Christian faith.[4] However, answering a survey question and living out a commitment to Christ and His teachings in everyday life are two different things. In Matthew 15:8 Jesus warned about people "who honor me with their lips, but their hearts are far from me."

Apathy and affluence can destroy a nation

It's not that the Israelites did not know God's standard; they just no longer cared enough to uphold it. As I read the prophecy of Amos, I can't help but notice the similarities between ancient Israel and modern America. Amos announced these strong words 800 years before the birth of Jesus, but his message is still relevant to America today because we are guilty of that same deadly mixture of apathy and affluence. Compared to the rest of the world, Americans are some of the wealthiest people alive today. Even the most modest homes seem like mansions when compared to other countries. Many Americans can also relate to having both a winter home and a summer home or a lake house. Theodore Roosevelt, who served as president at the beginning of the 20th century, cautioned Americans against becoming self-satisfied: "The things that will destroy America are prosperity-at-any-price, peace-at-any-price, safety-first instead of duty-first, the love of soft living and the get-rich-quick theory of life." These are sobering words from the perspective of a man whose face is on Mt. Rushmore alongside Washington, Jefferson and Lincoln.

Did you hear about the recent survey going on in America? People were asked, "What is the biggest problem in America, ignorance or apathy?" The number one answer was, "I don't know, and I don't care." I'm kidding, of course, but none of us should blame ignorance as a reason for inaction when it comes to changing the moral state of our country. We know what's happening, thanks to 24-hour news programming. However, if we aren't doing anything about it, the only other explanation is indifference—we just don't care.

Israel, largely unconcerned about how their society was disintegrating before their eyes, received a stern warning from Amos:

"Woe to you who are complacent in Zion, and to you who feel secure on Mount Samaria, you notable men of the foremost nation, to whom the people of Israel come!...You put off the evil day and bring near a reign of terror. You lie on beds inlaid with ivory and lounge on your couches. You dine on choice lambs and fattened calves. You strum away on your harps like David and improvise on musical instruments. You drink wine by the bowlful and use the finest lotions, but you do not grieve over the ruin of Joseph. Therefore you will be among the first to go into exile; your feasting and lounging will end." Amos 6:1, 3-7

If I could paraphrase that passage for America, it would read something like this:

"Woe to you who are apathetic and affluent in America. And to you who feel secure in your fine homes, you notable men, to whom conservative Christians look for advice. Think about history. Read the prophecies of Amos to Israel. Are you better than those people? You lie on your beds and relax on your recliners, clicking through the hundreds of channels on your flat screen. Every night you search for the next best restaurant, while passing by homeless people on the side of the road. You trust the money in your wallet and your smart 21st century technology more than you trust God. You do not help those who need help, while you live the American dream. Therefore, don't be surprised when you are stripped of your luxuries. Perhaps then you will seek God."

It's time to change course before it's too late. Christian families must join together against a rising tide of callousness in our nation and say like Joshua, "As for me and my house, we will serve the Lord." (Joshua 24:15) And let's prayerfully expand it further to say, "As for me and my country, we will be one nation under God!"

God sends a warning before He sends judgment

God sent Israel warning after warning, but they had ignored each one for years. Past events that they may have interpreted as a stroke of bad luck or strange coincidence were actually God's attempts to get their attention so they would turn to Him for help. In Amos 4:6 God said, "I gave you empty stomachs in every city and lack of bread in every town, yet you have not returned to me." God repeats this refrain five times. He draws their attention to the weather and points out, "I also withheld rain from you when the harvest was still three months away...yet you have not returned to me." (4:7-8) He then explains why they haven't seen the harvests they would like: "Many times I struck your gardens and vineyards...yet you have not returned to me." (4:9) He also explains, "I sent plagues among you as I did to

Egypt...yet you have not returned to me." (4:10) Finally God says that the time for warning was now over: "I overthrew some of you as I overthrew Sodom and Gomorrah. You were like a burning stick snatched from the fire, yet you have not returned to me...Therefore this is what I will do to you, Israel, and because I will do this to you, prepare to meet your God, O Israel." (4:11-12)

God is sending me, and plenty of other pastors, to warn our nation that judgment is coming unless Americans repent and return to God. As I look back on the last few decades in American history, I wonder how many times we have ignored God's warnings that came in the form of wars and disasters. It could be that God is saying to America:

"You went through two unwinnable wars in Korea and Vietnam, yet you did not return to me. Instead, you removed prayer and Bible reading from your schools.

"You went through the global embarrassment of having your embassy in Iran invaded and American citizens held as hostage for 444 days, and your rescue attempt crashed in the desert. And yet you did not return to me. Instead you legalized the killing of unborn babies.

"You've become the target of terrorism, and yet you did not return to me. Instead, you lead the world in the production and distribution of pornography.

"You faced the worst economic recession since the great depression and massive super storms several times after that. Yet you did not return to me. Instead, you decided to change my definition of marriage to what my Word calls an abomination.

"Therefore, America, prepare to meet your God."

Are we prepared to meet God? One day every American and every person on earth will die and stand before a holy God. Are you prepared for Him to ask you why you should be with Him in heaven? Would you point to the fact that you've done more good things than bad things in your life? If that's your answer to His question, you're not prepared. Or maybe you would say, "Let me into heaven because I'm better than most people." If that's your answer, you aren't ready to meet God either. However, you are prepared if at one time in your life you have honestly professed, "I'm a sinner. I can never be good enough to earn God's forgiveness. Instead, I trust Jesus Christ and the blood He shed for me on the cross. I confess that He is my Lord and my Savior." Do you see the difference? If you can answer that way, then you are prepared to meet God.

It's time for the Church to wake up

If you visit most liberal support group websites, you'll quickly see that they are passionate about changing our culture. In fact, they call their efforts a *movement.* Meanwhile, many Christians just yawn and change the channel on the television when they see what's happening in America today. The only "movement" they make is going from the couch to the refrigerator. Many Christians cannot get motivated to get out of bed to worship on Sunday mornings.

Do you care about the direction of our nation? Are you alarmed that our moral foundation has been cracking for the past few decades? The sad truth is that many Christians are not concerned enough to register to vote, much less let their voices be heard at the polls. According to the Pew Research Center, in 2015 there were about 62 million evangelical Christians in America.[5] In 2012, it's been estimated that less than half of all evangelicals voted in the presidential election.[6] Keith Green was one of my favorite Christian singers. Had he lived, we would be the same age today, but at twenty-eight Keith died in a plane crash in Garden Valley near my home in East Texas. In one of his most powerful songs called, "Asleep in the Light," Keith sounded much like an Old Testament prophet describing the Church contentedly sound asleep in the light of God.

God will restore any nation that returns to Him

By now you're probably thinking, "Do you have any good news for us?" Yes, I do. So did Amos. True to the prophet's predictions, the Assyrians would overrun the northern kingdom of Israel in 722 B.C., and the southern kingdom of Judah would fall next to the Babylonians in 587 B.C. It would look pretty bleak for a long time for God's people who were being punished for their disobedience. However, at the end of the book of Amos, the prophet also revealed that a day was coming that would change everything.

"In that day I will restore David's fallen tent. I will repair its broken places, restore its ruins, and build it as it used to be, so that they may possess the remnant of Edom and all the nations that bear my name," declares the Lord, who will do these things.

"The days are coming," declares the Lord, "when the reaper will be overtaken by the plowman and the planter by the one treading grapes. New wine will drip from the mountains and flow from all the hills. I will bring back my exiled people Israel; they will rebuild the ruined cities and live in them. They will plant vineyards and drink their wine; they will make gardens and eat their fruit."

"I will plant Israel in their own land, never again to be uprooted from the land I have given them," says the Lord your God. Amos 9:11-15

What day was Amos talking about when God would bring back the Jews "…never again to be uprooted"? Some commentaries indicate that God was talking about a time when the Jewish people later returned from exile and rebuilt the temple. However, read the passage carefully. It says the Jews would NEVER be uprooted again. We know from history that after they returned from exile, the Jews were uprooted again in 70 A.D. when the Romans utterly destroyed Jerusalem. In fact, they were dispersed across the globe for the next 1900 years! But at the beginning of the 20th century, Jews started returning to the Holy Land—drawn there like moths to a flame. Then in 1948 something happened that had seemed unlikely for ages—Israel became a nation again, just as God predicted in Amos.

Today they are back…NEVER again to be uprooted. I've witnessed firsthand the fulfillment of this scripture describing the resurgence of modern Israel. I've seen "David's tent restored," and I've seen the "ruins rebuilt." The scene Amos painted of rolling hills producing a bounty of crops and wine has been fulfilled in the miraculous agricultural revolution happening in Israel. Isn't it exciting to know that you're living in a time of fulfilled scripture? That realization should fan our faith in the possibility that it's not too late for us…if only we will repent and align ourselves once more with God's plumb line, His moral standard for living.

Prior to the election in 2012, the Billy Graham Evangelistic Association took out full-page ads in *The Wall Street Journal* and *USA Today* with an unprecedented statement from Billy Graham that read:

> "The legacy we leave behind for our children, grandchildren, and this great nation is crucial. As I approach my 94th birthday, I realize this election could be my last. I believe it is vitally important that we cast our ballots for candidates who base their decisions on biblical principles and support the nation of Israel. I urge you to vote for those who protect the sanctity

of life and support the biblical definition of marriage between a man and a woman. Vote for biblical values this November 6, and pray with me that America will remain one nation under God."

If I had a vote, we'd add Billy Graham's face up there beside the presidents on Mt. Rushmore! Christians must stand united for the issues that matter most, believing that God can and will restore any nation that returns to Him. Is time running out for America to turn around and repent? It's a serious question to consider because God has blessed America despite our unfaithfulness for many decades. When will He say He has had enough? Let's explore this question more in the next chapter.

.

CHAPTER 4

A Time of Grace in America

THERE HAS BEEN ONLY ONE TIME IN HISTORY WHEN ENEMY TROOPS HAVE OCCUPIED OUR CAPITAL CITY. By God's grace, we won the War of Independence when the British surrendered at Yorktown in 1781. However, they did not go quietly. Just a few years later they were back with a vengeance for the War of 1812. On August 24, 1814, British General Robert Ross attacked Washington D.C. on a hot, 100-degree summer August day. They overtook the city quickly and easily, partly because D.C. had only 8,000 residents (half of whom were slaves) and they presented little resistance.

When the British stormed the White House, they found that President James Madison and his First Lady, Dolley, had already fled to safety in nearby Georgetown with a famous portrait of George Washington and a copy of the Declaration of Independence in tow. According to historians, the enemy soldiers then brazenly sat down to eat the food left over from a presidential meal—even using the White House fine china—before ransacking the building and setting it ablaze, along with the Capitol and other official buildings.

The arsonists intended to carry out their deadly work the next day throughout D.C., but an unusual weather phenomenon brought their plans to a standstill and reduced their occupation of our capital to a mere 26 hours.[7] Although they seldom make landfall around Washington, a violent hurricane suddenly roared ashore—aimed directly at the British troops. For the next two hours, a flood of torrential rain and blustery winds quickly extinguished the still raging fires, saving the White House and other historical buildings from being totally destroyed. As if that weren't enough, several tornadoes spawned by the hurricane killed more British soldiers than the battle of Washington itself! The weather was so bad that General Ross decided to leave Washington and return to their ships.

Soaked to the skin in his uniform, a British admiral reportedly asked an American lady on the street, "Great God, Madame! Is this the kind of storm to which you are accustomed in this infernal country?" The lady answered, "No, Sir. This is a special interposition of Almighty God to drive our enemies from our city."[8]

You won't read in modern history books that God was behind the unusual atmospheric activity, but that storm probably turned the tide and made the difference between defeat and victory in the War of 1812. Had Washington burned to the ground and the British troops not been decimated, we might be loyal subjects of Queen Elizabeth to this day! But God intervened. Is there any question that He has blessed our nation from the very beginning? Despite the many times in our short history we have turned away from Him, He has continued to show us overwhelming love and grace.

There is a story in the Bible that reminds me of God's patient relationship with America. America isn't Israel, but we can recognize a recurring historical pattern in Israel's history that we also see in our nation. The book of Hosea in the Old Testament is about a prophet named Hosea who preached from his own personal experiences with his unfaithful wife. His story is an unusual word picture of God's steadfast relationship with wayward Israel. Like an episode of reality television, Hosea's life with Gomer unfolded in dramatic fashion. God told the Israelites that they were like Hosea's unfaithful wife; they were guilty of spiritual adultery. They had not only broken God's Law, but they had also broken God's heart. However, like a patient lover, God stood by Israel and offered His people another chance. It's easy to envision America in this story, playing the starring role of the stubborn wife who forgets about the one who loves her.

God's instructions to Hosea

Go back with me in your mind 2,800 years ago to a small village in Israel and the home of a young man named Hosea. God spoke to him one day and told him to get married. I imagine that Hosea, being a bachelor, probably smiled at this idea and said, "Sure thing, Lord! Whatever you say!"

Then God continued, "And I have just the girl picked out for you—her name is Gomer." Hosea must have really grinned at this revelation because he had heard that Gomer was a gorgeous girl whom every man wanted. But then God said something that took the wind out of his sails. "By the way," He added, "Gomer is a prostitute, but I want you to marry her anyway." Before Hosea could take a breath and object, God revealed something else about his bride-to-be. "Hosea," He said, "your wife is going to be unfaithful to you and to your children."

Did Hosea hear God right? Talk about disappointment and confusion! Most of us will admit that God sometimes tells us to do strange things that don't make sense at the time. It takes extraordinary faith to move forward when we don't understand what God is doing, but Hosea was no ordinary young man. He readily obeyed the Lord and went ahead and married Gomer, even though he knew all about her true character. Maybe he hoped his love for her would prevent her from returning to a life of prostitution. Maybe he thought things could change. In any case, they soon had three children—two boys and a girl—but Hosea's home life grew worse every day.

God's love is persistent

In the following biblical account, God substitutes the names of Hosea's family to create the vivid imagery of escalating unfaithfulness between God and His people.

> When the Lord began to speak through Hosea, the Lord said to him, "Go, take to yourself an adulterous wife and children of unfaithfulness, because the land is guilty of the vilest adultery in departing from the Lord." So he married Gomer daughter of Diblaim, and she conceived and bore him a son. Then the Lord said to Hosea, "Call him Jezreel, because I will soon punish the house of Jehu for the massacre at Jezreel, and I will put an end to the kingdom of Israel. In that day I will break Israel's bow in the Valley of Jezreel."
>
> Gomer conceived again and gave birth to a daughter. Then the Lord said to Hosea, "Call her Lo-Ruhamah, for I will no longer show love to the house of Israel, that I should at all forgive them. Yet I will show love to the house of Judah; and I will save them—not by bow, sword or battle, or by horses and

horsemen, but by the Lord their God."

After she had weaned Lo-Ruhamah, Gomer had another son. Then the Lord said, "Call him Lo-Ammi, for you are not my people, and I am not your God."
Hosea 1:2-8

One morning Hosea walked into the kitchen and found a "Dear Hosea" letter on the table. As he picked up the letter and read it, I imagine Gomer may have told him something like this:

Dear Hosea,

I'm no longer fulfilled as a wife and a mother. It's not you—it's me. I feel trapped. I want to live. I want to love. I want to laugh. I'm leaving you and the kids and returning to my former profession.

Don't try to find me. It's over, Hosea.

Goodbye.

For some, Hosea's situation is all too real. You know exactly how rejection feels. We don't know how long Gomer was separated from Hosea, and we don't know how many men she welcomed into her arms. However, her life soon spiraled completely out of control because she eventually sold herself into slavery. She sank so low that she became nothing but property to be bought and sold by evil men.

At this point in the story, Hosea may have thought to himself, "Well, that's that. I did what the Lord said—and it turned out exactly the way He told me it would." However, the story was far from over. The Lord gave Hosea instructions again—and this time he could hardly believe his ears.

God has to illustrate grace so we'll understand it

What God said next confused Hosea even more because He wanted
Hosea to go to the slave auction block prepared to buy back his own wife!

> The Lord said to me, "Go, show your love to your
> wife again, though she is loved by another and is an
> adulteress. Love her as the Lord loves the Israelites,
> though they turn to other gods and love the sacred
> raisin cakes." So I bought her for fifteen shekels of silver
> and about a homer and a lethek of barley.* Then I told
> her, "You are to live with me many days; you must not
> be a prostitute or be intimate with any man, and I will
> live with you." *about a bushel and a half* Hosea 3:1-3

Hosea scraped together all the money he could find, and then
in desperation he even shouldered a bushel and a half of grain and
made his way toward town. In accordance with the customs of that
day, Gomer and all the other slaves were stripped naked by the slave
masters so that potential buyers could see exactly what they were
bidding on. Hosea must have hardly recognized his wife because of
the physical toll sin and shame had taken on her. But before he could
catch her eye in the crowd, the bidding began.

In my imagination I think the next scene unfolds with one
man yelling out, "Ten pieces of silver!" and then Hosea hurriedly
saying, "Eleven!"

Another man says, "Twelve pieces of silver."

Hosea, his nerves shot, gulps and adds, "Thirteen!"

"Fourteen pieces of silver!" comes the quick retort.

Hosea counters, "Fifteen pieces of silver!"

Then everyone drops out because that was a high price to pay for
a slave. One remaining man is still in the fight, for he says, "I'll give
you 15 pieces of silver and a bushel of barley!" Silence falls over the

crowd. Then Hosea clears his throat and says, "I'll give you fifteen pieces of silver and a bushel-and-a-half of barley!"

The other man waves his hand and snorts, "You can have her. She's not worth that much, anyway."

To that, the auctioneer says, "Sold!"

Now that Hosea had her, what would he do? According to the Mosaic Law, he had the right to accuse her publicly and have her stoned to death. That would have restored his public standing as a man of righteousness. Or he could have taken her home and said to her harshly, "You lived like a slave, so I'm going to make you a slave. You're going to work your fingers to the bone from morning to night to repay what it cost me to buy you."

Instead, Hosea resisted his natural human desire for revenge and obeyed God's instructions to welcome her back home. I envision him tenderly approaching Gomer, wrapping his robe around her nakedness and saying softly, "Sweetheart, I know what you've done, and I forgive you. I still love you. Will you come back home and be my wife and a mother to our children?"

It sounds unlikely, doesn't it? He did not treat wayward Gomer as she deserved—that would be justice. He gave her instead what she really needed most—that's grace. Grace is one of the most difficult concepts for our human minds to understand, so God chose to illustrate it throughout Scripture with stories like Hosea. Even Hosea's name is a derivative of the name "Jesus." Jesus is God's masterpiece portrait of grace—dying for our sins, even though we did not deserve to be saved. That's how great His love is for us.

America started out strong

Hosea pointed out how God blessed Israel from its inception. Israel's humble beginnings are similar to our own, starting out as a bedraggled group escaping slavery in Egypt. God provided for their every need while they were in the desert searching for the Promised Land on their way to becoming a full-fledged nation. God not only relates to individuals; He relates to nations on a personal and intimate level. He says, "When Israel was a child, I loved him...I led them with cords of human kindness, with ties of love; I lifted the yoke from their neck and bent down to feed them." (Hosea 11:1, 4)

The same can be said of America in that God blessed our nation from its birth, but we used to depend much more on Him than we openly do today. For example, Americans are familiar with the date July 4, 1776, the signing of the Declaration of Independence. But do you know what happened exactly 40 days before that event on May 17, 1776? The Continental Congress called citizens to an extended period of fasting and prayer—and only at the end of the solemn 40 days of prayer did they sign the Declaration of Independence. Consider what it would take for our modern Congress to call for a similar event!

The style of English language in this proclamation may be old, but their intention is clear and relevant:

> "Desirous to have people of all ranks and degrees duly impressed with a solemn sense of God's superintending providence, and of their duty, devoutly to rely, in all their lawful enterprizes, on His aid and direction, do earnestly recommend, that Friday, the Seventeenth day of May next [40 days before July 4], be observed by the said colonies as **a day of humiliation, fasting, and prayer; that we may, with united hearts, confess and bewail our manifold sins and transgressions, and, by a sincere repentance and amendment of life, appease His righteous displeasure, and, through the merits and mediation of Jesus Christ, obtain His pardon and forgiveness;** humbly imploring His assistance to frustrate the

cruel purposes of our unnatural enemies... it is recommended to Christians of all denominations, to assemble for public worship, and abstain from servile labour on the said day."

God blessed our young nation's commitment to serve and honor Him through consecrated events like this. And yet, the historical pattern is one of taking three steps forward and two steps back in our spiritual progress, as it was for Israel in Hosea's time. See if his description of Israel 2,800 years ago doesn't sound like our American culture today:

> The Lord has a charge to bring against you who live in the land: "There is no faithfulness, no love, no acknowledgment of God in the land. There is only cursing, lying and murder, stealing and adultery; they break all bounds, and bloodshed follows bloodshed."
> Hosea 4:1-2

One of the ways we have forsaken God's moral law and principles is with landmark rulings in the 20th and 21st centuries on prayer, abortion and marriage that significantly altered the trajectory of our nation.

God has a definition of marriage

The latest ruling occurred in 2015 when we culminated the process of redefining a 4,000-year-old definition of marriage that had spanned almost every culture on earth since its inception. The vast majority of cultures throughout the world have long recognized marriage as a permanent union between one man and one woman. God holds the patent on marriage because He invented it. The very first marriage was between Adam and Eve in the Garden of Eden when He brought them together for companionship and to populate the planet. His original design was and always will be one man and one woman united until death. "At the beginning of creation God 'made them male and female.' For this reason a man will leave his father and mother and be united to his wife and the two will become one flesh. So they are no longer two, but one. Therefore what God has joined together, let man not separate." (Mark 10:6-9)

However, humanity corrupted God's original design for marriage. In the first few chapters of Genesis, all kinds of evil and wickedness unraveled among the people, and much of it had to do with the perversion of God's plan for one woman and one man. Just before God destroyed the world with the flood the Bible says, "God saw how corrupt the earth had become, for all the people on earth had corrupted their ways." (Genesis 6:12)

In reading the Old Testament, it's obvious some of the men had multiple wives. The first man to have more than one wife was Lamech. "He took two wives." (Genesis 4:19) God didn't *give* him two. King Solomon wrote, "He who finds a wife finds what is good." (Proverbs 18:22) He had too much of a good thing because we read in 1 Kings 11:3 that Solomon had 700 royal wives and 300 concubines (and 1,000 mothers-in-law!). The Bible says Solomon's many wives turned his heart away from God. God never commanded polygamy; it was a practice that reflected the sinfulness of the hearts of humanity. By the New Testament period, it is clear God's standard of one woman and one man had been restored because this was the specific requirement for pastors and deacons.

However, humanity continued to pervert God's definition of marriage throughout history, culminating in the U.S. in the 1970s with the advent of no-fault divorce and same sex marriage in the 21st century. It was not too long ago in 1996 that our government passed the Defense of Marriage Act that defined marriage as a legal union between one man and one woman. It passed by overwhelming majorities in both the Senate and the House (85-14 in the Senate and 342-67 in the House). President Clinton signed the bill into law. However, in 2011 the Obama administration told the Justice Department not to defend this law. They proposed that it be repealed and replaced with the Respect for Marriage Act in order to recognize a same-sex union as marriage. Fast forward to the summer of 2015 when the Supreme Court made same-sex marriage the law of the land.

Homosexual behavior is nothing new. It was practiced in Sodom and Gomorrah. It was practiced in the Greek and Roman cultures. Emperor Nero married two different men. Later when Christianity spread into the Roman Empire, same-sex marriage was outlawed. In the span of just a few years, public opinion in the U.S. has changed dramatically on the issue of same-sex marriage. There are several outspoken politicians, including at least one president, who are on the record as having been against same-sex marriage, only to reverse this position later.

The reason I believe same-sex marriage is a corruption of God's design is because I believe the Bible teaches that same-sex behavior is sinful. That said, biblical arguments will never change the mind of many who practice homosexual behavior. They have answers for every point. But when Christians show them the unconditional love of Jesus, they have no rebuttal. Those who disagree with the Bible about same-sex marriage are our neighbors and sometimes our family members. Jesus said to love our neighbors. Some of them are hostile to Christians and label us as bigoted, narrow-minded homophobes. They see us as their enemies. Jesus told us to love our enemies and to pray for them. If you know people who disagree with you about this matter, don't talk AT them; talk WITH them and listen honestly to why they believe what they do. You must earn the right to share your opinion. You can love them without condoning their behavior.

Some people argue that we're living in different times and that these modern times call for modern morality. Notice I am making a distinction between homosexual tendencies and homosexual behavior. I'm not attacking homosexuals. God loves homosexuals. But when any culture puts its official stamp of approval on what the Bible calls sin, it is an indication of how far it has wandered from God's Word.

Standing up for life

In my opinion the issue of same-sex unions pales in comparison to the horrific sin of abortion. Before Roe v. Wade, abortion was a crime. In 1973 our nation legalized the killing of a baby in the womb. Again, abortions aren't new. Pharaoh himself ordered the midwives to abort baby boys in ancient Egypt as a means of population control. Prior to legal abortion, doctors and non-licensed medical "professionals" in the United States had performed them for decades.

There are three victims of every abortion: a child, a mother and a father. Parents who choose to abort a child struggle with the emotional fallout for the rest of their lives. The church where I serve is one of a growing number of churches in America with an abortion recovery ministry. Abortion is a double tragedy. It not only stops a beating heart, but it destroys human potential. We have missed the impact of the lives of those millions of Americans who never had a chance to live outside the womb. Who knows? The next Albert Einstein, Mother Teresa or Billy Graham might have been among the babies we have aborted in the past few decades.

When some Christians heard of the Supreme Court's ruling on gay marriage, they despaired and thought, "This is surely the end." However, compare this ruling to the Roe v. Wade decision in 1973. Was that the end of the pro-life movement? No, it was a wake-up call to those who supported the right to life. Since that ruling, millions of people have been energized and mobilized to stand up for the unborn. Has it worked? Abortion is still legal, and the number of abortions peaked in 1981, but they have been declining. The year 2015 marked the fewest abortions performed in America since Roe v. Wade. The ruling on gay marriage can also serve to fuel even greater support for traditional marriage between a man and a woman.

Our only hope is to return to God!

Thankfully, Hosea offers a ray of hope in this dark scene of rebellion by predicting Israel will have a surprising change of heart. "Afterward the Israelites will return and seek the Lord their God and David their king. They will come trembling to the Lord and to his blessings in the last days." (Hosea 3:5) His instructions to Israel are the same words that we need to follow:

> Return, O Israel, to the Lord your God. Your sins
> have been your downfall! Take words with you and
> return to the Lord. Say to him: "Forgive all our sins
> and receive us graciously." Hosea 14:1-2

Despite everything they had done, God was still willing to draw the people back to His heart, the same way Hosea received Gomer. The message for us is that it's not too late, America! There is still time to return to God. I love the picture God portrays of drawing aside an entire nation so He can heal its wounds and restore joy to the people:

> God said, "Therefore I am now going to allure her;
> I will lead her into the desert and speak tenderly to
> her. There I will give her back her vineyards and will
> make the Valley of Achor a door of hope. There she
> will sing as in the days of her youth." (Hosea 2:14-15)

The valley of Achor was a familiar reference to a tragic story in the Old Testament. It was the location where Joshua had directed the Hebrews to stone Achan and his family because he had been stealing and lying. In other words, Achor was a place of miserable memories, but God would soon turn misery into a miracle. Instead of shame, there would be singing and joyful music.

God wants to offer America a doorway of hope as well, but we must choose to go through it. In spite of our problems, which I attempt to spell out very plainly in this book, I am equally hopeful for our nation. A few years ago I wrote a book called, *H.O.P.E. When You Need it the Most*. It includes a chapter about having Hope for America where H.O.P.E. stands for Having Only Positive Expectations. I have only positive expectations for our nation and our future. Regardless of who is elected in 2016 and 2020 and 2024, there is still hope for America. Our nation's return to God won't start in the White House, the courthouse, the statehouse or the jailhouse; it's going to start in the church house with God's people. Our hope is not dependent upon the one sitting in the Oval Office in Washington. Our hope is found in the One who is sitting on the throne of heaven. Governments change; cultures change; laws change. But Jesus Christ is the same yesterday, today and forever.

God loves you so much that He paid the highest price

I can't conclude a lesson about Hosea without presenting the final and most important truth. And it's this: God loves you. He always has, and He always will. Hosea is one of my favorite prophets because his life and marriage is a living parable of God's love and grace. Hosea went to a slave auction and paid everything he had to redeem Gomer. Jesus came into the world and paid everything He had to redeem you. The Bible says, "It was not with perishable things such as silver or gold that you were redeemed from the empty way of life handed down to you from your forefathers, but with the precious blood of Christ, a lamb without blemish or defect." (1 Peter 1:18-19) At the cross Jesus bid the silver of His tears and the gold of His blood to buy us back, even though we were unfaithful sinners.

God knows the very worst about each of us, yet He loves us more than we can ever imagine. Some may read the story of Hosea and Gomer and say, "I couldn't love a husband or wife who was repeatedly unfaithful to me!" However, remember Hosea was acting out God's remarkable love for us! When you marry someone, you don't get a marriage; you get a mate. When you become a Christian, you don't receive a religion; you receive a living relationship with a Savior. God said, "I am the Lord your God, who brought you out of Egypt. You shall acknowledge no God but me, no Savior except me." (Hosea

13:4) There is only one name under heaven whereby you can be saved, and that is the name of Jesus.

The Future of America

America is at a crossroads. We know through the story of Hosea and hundreds of other promises throughout God's Word that He will accept and forgive all who genuinely repent and come back to Him. However, He is just as clear about the repercussions of continued disobedience. I don't know if America is at a point yet where she is ready to fall to her knees in prayer and beg God for forgiveness. I pray we will get there before it's too late—but no one can predict the future. What if we don't repent? What happens then? We'll explore the worst-case scenario in the next chapter as we consider the possibility that America could even now be under God's curse.

CHAPTER 5

Could God Ever Curse America?

THESE ARE FAR FROM THE DARKEST DAYS OF OUR NATION. As a student of American history, I believe the worst chapter in our nation's past was the bloody Civil War that pitted brother against brother, killed 620,000 Americans and injured millions more. President Lincoln, who served at the helm of our nation during that tragedy, gave a pivotal address as he was sworn into office for the second time as the War was winding down. I believe this second inaugural address, delivered on March 4, 1865, was his finest speech—although it reads more like a sermon than a presidential address. At only four minutes, it was the second shortest inaugural speech ever given by a U.S. president. (The shortest was George Washington's second inaugural address, barely two minutes in length.)

Picture the scene where this fateful address took place. The Civil War was nearly over. General Robert E. Lee would surrender a month after Lincoln's speech. Five days after Lee's surrender, Lincoln would be dead from an assassin's bullet.

You may read the speech in its entirety if you visit the Lincoln Memorial in Washington where his words are engraved there in stone. (Incidentally, his speech contains six biblical references and two quotes from Jesus.) Lincoln insightfully understood that the War itself was part of the judgment of God against America, and he explained it this way:

> "The Almighty has His own purposes. 'Woe unto the world because of offenses; for it must needs be that offenses come, but woe to that man by whom the offense cometh.' (Matthew 18:7) If we shall suppose that American slavery is one of those offenses which, in the providence of God, He now wills to remove, and that He gives to both North and South this terrible war as the woe due to those by whom the offense came, shall we discern therein any departure from those divine attributes which the believers in a living God always ascribe to Him? Fondly do we hope, fervently do we pray, that this mighty scourge of war may speedily pass away. Yet, if God wills that it continue until all the wealth piled by the bondsman's two hundred and fifty years of unrequited toil shall be sunk, and until every drop of blood drawn with the lash shall be paid by another drawn with the sword, as was said three thousand years ago, so still it must be said 'the judgments of the Lord are true and righteous altogether.'" (Psalm 19:9)

–March 4, 1865

In other words, if God deemed it proper to simply wipe America off the face of the earth, then, Lincoln agreed, that was His Divine right to do so. Thankfully, God had other plans for America, and our nation survived that test. However, today we hear the rumblings of a second civil war, but this one will not be fought with rifles and cannons. It is a moral battle fought with convictions. The lines are clearly drawn, and the single overarching issue at stake asks a fairly simple question. Will our nation continue to use biblical morality as our guide as we have from our founding?

God may issue a different kind of judgment on America

How do you think Americans would react if tomorrow's news headlines announced God's judgment unless we repented? Twitter would blow up and the backlash might break the Internet permanently. But what would God's judgment on America look like today? Jesus said this about ancient cities such as Korazin and Bethsaida that outright rejected His ministry, "Woe unto you…for if the miracles had been done in Tyre and Sidon had been performed in you, they would have repented in sackcloth and ashes." (Matthew 11:21) Notice Jesus didn't call down the fire of judgment on those cities. He didn't actually curse them. He simply predicted that "bad news" or "woe" would happen in the future as a consequence of their moral and spiritual climate. True to His word, these cities gradually sank into historical insignificance. While biblical cities throughout the Galilee areas such as Cana and Tiberius continue to exist today as thriving communities, Korazin and Bethsaida are only ruins.

We are facing dangerous and scary times as a nation as we continue to slide down a slippery slope of moral depravity. God's judgment against America may not come as a fiery conflagration like some people imagine. Instead, it may come in the form of a gradual decline from within that eventually leads to

America becoming a wasteland. I don't mean America will become a Hollywood version of a Mad Max movie, although that is certainly possible. I mean a moral and spiritual wasteland.

In fact, we may already be seeing evidence of this kind of judgment. For example, America no longer holds the moral high ground in world affairs because, among other things, we are the leader in exporting violence and pornography. Our influence as a Christian nation is waning while revival is breaking out in many places throughout the world today. Thousands in other countries are responding to the Gospel every day in what appears to be another Great Awakening. Do we see spiritual revival on that scale happening in America today?

God may not use a foreign army to judge America as He did for Israel in biblical times. Moral decay and decline will destroy a nation from within just as certainly as an invading army; it just happens slowly. More houses have been destroyed from termites within than from tornados from the outside.

God's charge against America

Once again, we can return to God's Word to find insights on the current state of our nation. Although the book of Malachi was written over 2,400 years ago, moral conditions were much the same as they are in America today. "Malachi" is the Hebrew word translated "angel," but that's not how the Jews saw Malachi when he warned them that they better repent. From their perspective they were cruising along just fine. They had already spent several generations in exile, as the prophet Amos had predicted. Only 100 years had passed since they had been granted the opportunity to return to their land and rebuild the temple during a time of revival under Nehemiah. Yet, in the words of Bible scholar, Charles Ryrie, "the initial enthusiasm had worn off" by the time Malachi came on the scene.[9]

The thrill of revival was long gone, but still the people doggedly pointed to their good deeds and religious rituals when Malachi challenged them. "What are we doing wrong?" they argued. Even the most religious among them seemed oblivious to God's charges. Consider this back-and-forth dialogue between God and the priests:

> But you ask, "How have we shown contempt for your name?"
>
> [God responds] "You place defiled food on my altar."
>
> But you ask, "How have we defiled you?"
>
> [God responds] "By saying that the Lord's table is contemptible." Malachi 1:6-7

In fact, the whole format of this short prophecy in the Old Testament reads like a debate between God and the people. God speaks to them about their sin, and they respond with eight argumentative questions.

Like the people in Malachi, when we are confronted we want to point to all the good things we are doing as a nation—and there are many—but what specific charges could God bring against us? Billy Graham shares a story about his wife, Ruth Bell, after she reviewed a draft of a manuscript he was writing about the downward spiral of America's morality. According to Graham, she put down the manuscript and surprised him by saying God would "owe an apology" to Sodom and Gomorrah if He didn't bring His judgment on America—and soon![10]

Malachi points out at least two important indictments that signal when a culture is on the brink of destruction.

1. **A culture in moral decline experiences prevalent divorce**

   In Malachi God speaks clearly about His position on divorce.

   > Another thing you do: You flood the Lord's altar with tears. You weep and wail because he no longer pays attention

to your offerings or accepts them with pleasure from your hands. You ask, "Why?" It is because the Lord is acting as the witness between you and the wife of your youth, because you have broken faith with her, though she is your partner, the wife of your marriage covenant. Has not the Lord made them one? In flesh and spirit they are his. And why one? Because he was seeking godly offspring. So guard yourself in your spirit, and do not break faith with the wife of your youth. I hate divorce,' says the Lord Almighty…" Malachi 2:13-16

God hates divorce because it is a sin; it is the breaking of a vow. Some of you are thinking, "I'm divorced. Does God hate *me* because I got a divorce?" Please understand—God hates divorce, but He loves people who have gone through the heartbreak of divorce. God hates the sin, but He loves the sinner. We have a hard time making that distinction sometimes, but God doesn't.

The introduction of no-fault divorce sabotaged God's perfect design for marriage. Up until the 1970s it was rather difficult to get a divorce in the United States. A party had to show "cause" for divorce, like adultery or abuse. I think the term "no-fault divorce" is the classic oxymoron (when words cancel each other out like "jumbo shrimp," "cruel joke," or "affordable health care"). Divorce is always someone's fault. Today a couple can petition for divorce for the simple reason of "incompatibility." I've been married for over 40 years, and I'm the first to admit that men and women are naturally incompatible. We are different by nature, and I say, "Vive la différence."

I believe that one of the most dangerous misconceptions in America today is the belief that by undoing "outdated" biblical morality, we are finally on our way to a better, more loving and tolerant society. However, the facts indicate otherwise. In 1960 the divorce rate in the U.S. was about 9%. Since the advent of no-fault divorce laws, the divorce rate spiked in the 1980s at 24% and was at about 19% in 2015 (more and more couples are living together without getting married, so divorces aren't reported in these relationships). In the 1950s, for every seven marriages, there was one divorce. You've likely heard the statistic that "half of marriages end in divorce"—that is a false and misleading statement. It is true that for every two new marriages, there is one divorce in the U.S., but that number doesn't take into consideration the 54 million marriages that remain intact.[11] Although divorce is still far too prevalent, it is more accurate to say that for every three intact marriages, there is one marriage that ends in divorce.

God hates divorce because He realizes the extent of the damage it does. Marriage has always been the building block of a society. Before there was a nation or a church, there was a marriage. Divorce hurts a society because divorce hurts the people within the society. Divorce crushes a husband and a wife. Divorce wounds children. Many people carry the invisible scars of divorce. That's why many churches offer a divorce recovery ministries to rediscover the grace and forgiveness of God. Instead of emphasizing the damage of divorce in church, I find that it helps people to focus on what it takes to stay married. Jesus said that every marriage is made in heaven when He commanded, "…let no one split apart what God has joined together." (Mark 10:9, NLT) Malachi said God "is acting as the witness" between a husband and a wife, and it is one of His miracles that He creates one unit out of two different people. Henry Ford, who became one of the richest men in America by making the Model T Ford, also gave some great marriage advice. He said, "It's just the same as in the automobile business. Stick to one model!"

2. A culture in moral decline becomes increasingly self-centered

The people during Malachi's time had also stopped offering God the first and the best of their sacrifices because they wanted to keep more for themselves. In the first chapter God has this to say about their cheapskate worship habits. "'When you bring blind animals for sacrifice, is that not wrong? When you sacrifice crippled or diseased animals, is that not wrong? Try offering them to your governor! Would he be pleased with you? Would he accept you?' says the Lord

Almighty." (Malachi 1:8) Then God illustrates what true sacrificial giving is supposed to look like:

> Will a man rob God? Yet you rob me. But you ask, "How do we rob you?" "In tithes and offerings. You are under a curse—the whole nation of you—because you are robbing me. Bring the whole tithe into the storehouse, that there may be food in my house. Test me in this," says the Lord Almighty, "and see if I will not throw open the floodgates of heaven and pour out so much blessing that you will not have room enough for it. I will prevent pests from devouring your crops, and the vines in your fields will not cast their fruit," says the Lord Almighty. "Then all the nations will call you blessed, for yours will be a delightful land," says the Lord Almighty. Malachi 3:8-12

The word "tithe" isn't a religious word. It just means one-tenth. It's like the word "half" or "quarter." There's nothing particularly holy about the word—it's just a measurement. The principle of tithing is based on the fact that God owns everything; we own nothing. He lets us manage some of His wealth, and He asks us to acknowledge His ownership by giving back to Him at least one-tenth of the wealth He gives us. It's not a matter of legalistically figuring it out to the penny; tithing is a matter of joyfully expressing love.

Dr. Elmer Towns, in his book *Praying The Lord's Prayer for Spiritual Breakthrough*, tells a story about a time a father took his four-year-old son to McDonald's to have some father-son time. "Jimmy" asked his dad for some French fries. "Don" loved his son so much that he super-sized the fries and bought him a drink as well. They sat down and after a short prayer, Jimmy tore into the fries his dad placed in front of him. Don was smiling at how much a little boy could enjoy such a simple pleasure as hot, crispy French fries.

When the father reached over to taste one, Jimmy quickly put his arms around the fries making a little fence, pulled them toward himself and announced, "No! These are MINE!"

Don was in shock for a moment and couldn't believe Jimmy's selfish attitude. But instead of reprimanding him, he simply pulled his hand away and quietly reflected on Jimmy's behavior. He thought, "My son doesn't recognize that I am the source of those French fries. I was the one who took out my wallet and bought them." He smiled as he continued to ponder Jimmy's attitude. "And Jimmy doesn't realize that I'm six feet tall and weigh 200 pounds, and if I wanted to, I could easily take those fries away from his small hands. And he doesn't know that I really don't NEED his fries. I have enough money to go back to the counter and buy 30 servings of fries, more than he and I could ever eat."

Don wasn't hungry for fries. He simply wanted his son to invite him into his world by offering to share his blessing, the very blessing that he had provided in the first place.

Then Don realized what God was trying to teach him. Our heavenly Father supplies every blessing we have. He loves us so much that He desires for us to invite Him to sit down with us at our table and share the blessing He has provided. But too often we're like Jimmy and we say, "No, God, this is MINE!" We build our own little fences around our blessings and try to keep them to ourselves.

God doesn't need our French fries or our money. But it's an honor and a privilege for us to share our blessings with the One who gave them to us. When you give back to Him what is already His, He promises to open the windows of heaven and pour out more and more blessings—too much for you to contain.

It's human nature to be selfish. However, left unchecked, selfishness can ultimately destroy a society because we are too inwardly focused to care about God or others. Beware of becoming so self-centered about your own needs that you lose your ability to joyfully give back to God.

Let's review the charges God could bring against America.

Malachi describes an ancient biblical society infiltrated by divorce and a me-first mentality that no longer acknowledges God as the source of its blessings. America is suffering from the same maladies today. So what can we do to remedy the problems we are facing? Malachi provides some timeless insight there, too.

We need to accept God's message of love

God approached the problem like any good father does when he has to discipline his children by first reassuring the people that He loves them. However, they are so resistant to criticism that they want to argue with Him even about that fact! In the opening chapter of Malachi, God says:

> "I have loved you," says the Lord. "But you ask, 'How have you loved us?' Was not Esau Jacob's brother?' The Lord says. 'Yet I have loved Jacob, but Esau I have hated, and I have turned his mountains into a wasteland and left his inheritance to the desert jackals.'" Malachi 1:2-3

God isn't speaking about two individuals; He's talking about two nations—Edom and Israel. The descendants of Esau settled the nation of Edom and became very bitter toward God and entirely rejected His love. Is it any wonder that God preferred the descendants of Jacob who honored Him? Jacob and Esau were twins. God had informed their mother, Rebekah, before they were born that the younger one would rule over the older one. Esau was born first, and he was covered with hair, so they named him "hairy"—that's what Esau means in Hebrew. But Jacob was born holding on to his brother's heel, so they named him Jacob or "grabber."

The culture of that time dictated that Esau receive the birthright and the blessing as the firstborn son. But Jacob grabbed both of those away. He bought the birthright from Esau for a bowl of chili, and then he deceived his father, Isaac, into giving him the blessing.

When I read the words, "I have loved Jacob, but Esau I have hated," I don't stumble over the part about God hating Esau. I stumble over the part about God loving Jacob! How could God love *Jacob*? He was a crooked, conniving, lying, scoundrel of a grabber. Yet God loved him. If God can love a grabber like Jacob, I know He can love a sinner like me because His love is based on His grace, not our worthiness.

Some people think the doctrine of the love of God only appears in the New Testament. They make uninformed blanket statements like, "In the Old Testament, God is a God of wrath, but in the New Testament, He is a God of love." However, the God of the Old Testament is the very same God of the New Testament. In fact God says in Malachi 3:6, "I the Lord do not change." God doesn't love America—He loves Americans. If you accept His love like Jacob, you will be blessed. But if you are bitter and reject His love like Esau, you will miss out on His blessings. God gives Americans— and every person in every nation—a choice. What will you do about God's love for you?

We need to honor God's name

The second remedy Malachi presents to a nation in trouble is to once again honor God's name. Most Americans don't think it's important to attend worship on Sunday mornings. However, the Bible promises a special blessing to those who come together and honor the name of the Lord. The Bible says in Malachi 3 that after the people finally realized they were wrong and the Lord was right, they held a special ceremony of recommitment. "Then those who feared the Lord talked with each other, and the Lord listened and heard. A scroll of remembrance was written in his presence concerning those who feared the Lord and honored his name. 'They will be mine,' says the Lord Almighty, 'in the day when I make up my treasured possession.'" (Malachi 3:16-17)

According to this scripture, God keeps a written record of those who fear Him and honor His name. He considers them His treasured possession! What do you treasure most in your home? Every summer as wildfires rage around our country, we see people on the news being told to evacuate their homes immediately, leaving little time to gather their valuables. But do you know what they usually take? They do not grab the big screen TV or the expensive lamps. They usually take their photos. This passage portrays God with a heavenly "photo album" of believers gathering together to celebrate His greatness and to honor His holy name. When the people of God gather to worship, it isn't a Sunday morning routine. It is vital to our relationship with God. If you travel to Europe, you'll notice that there are plenty of churches, but they are largely empty. I fear that the same could be said of America one day.

America and the curse of sin

If God punishes disobedience, why do the wicked people in America often seem to have the upper hand? Throughout the Bible, the question is repeated, "Why do the wicked prosper?" The flip side of that question is, "Why do the righteous suffer?" The Bible teaches that there will be a day of reckoning when the righteous will be rewarded, and the wicked will be punished. Here's how God describes that day:

> "Surely the day is coming; it will burn like a furnace. All the arrogant and every evildoer will be stubble, and that day that is coming will set them on fire," says the Lord Almighty. "Not a root or a branch will be left to them. But for you who revere my name, the sun of righteousness will rise with healing in its wings. And you will go out and leap like calves released from the stall." Malachi 4:1-2

We won't be rewarded for any righteous acts we have done.

The Bible says our righteousness is like filthy rags—good for nothing. Jesus is our righteousness, and when we stand dressed in His righteousness, we are declared "right" in the sight of God. That is what sets us free and makes us feel like leaping and dancing, as Malachi describes. I love the image he uses of a calf released from a stall. No animal wants to be penned up, especially a young, rambunctious calf. This is a picture of how Jesus releases us from the bondage or curse of sin to embrace a new life of uncontained joy.

Here's a trivia question for you. What is the last word in the Old Testament? It's in the last chapter of Malachi: "See, I will send you the prophet Elijah before that great and dreadful day of the Lord comes. He will turn the hearts of the fathers to their children, and the hearts of the children to their fathers; or else I will come and strike the land with a **curse**." (Malachi 4:5-6)

"Curse" is a great one-word summary of the Old Testament. As I have studied the Bible carefully over the past four decades, I'm more convinced than ever that it is the Word of God. Although it contains 66 books penned by 40 men over a period of 1,600 years, it has an amazing unity and cohesiveness. It also has a single theme: the redemption of sinful humanity. In the beginning of the Old Testament, God created the heavens and the earth and put us in Paradise. But because of our foolish choices (expressed through Adam and Eve), we were kicked out of Paradise and fell under the curse of sin. The first human tears were shed, as were the first drops of blood.

But what Adam messed up, Jesus fixed up! The entire story of the Bible is about why and how God sent His only Son to remove the curse of sin. Curse may be the last word of the Old Testament, but when we turn to the very last page of the New Testament, we read these wonderful words: "**No longer will there be any curse.** The throne of God and of the Lamb will be in the city, and his servants will serve him. They will see his face, and his name will be on their foreheads." (Revelation 22:3-4)

We'll be invited back into Paradise where the Tree of Life grows. He will then wipe away every tear from our eyes. The Old Testament says, "Someone is coming." The New Testament tells us, "Someone has come—His name is Jesus." Revelation promises, "Someone is coming again."

Is America under a curse? Every person in America who has not accepted Christ as his or her Savior is still under the curse of sin. They cannot save themselves—they must be released from sin's grasp by Someone stronger than they are.

Even a blessed nation can go off course

The story of America is unfolding every day, and the next chapter remains to be seen. America isn't Israel, but we've seen there are some striking similarities in their history that cannot be ignored. God said He would bless those who bless Israel and curse those who curse Israel (Genesis 12:3). For this reason, if America knows what is good for her, she will always be the friend and ally of Israel. That's not a political statement; it's a biblical statement.

God blessed the nation of Israel above all the nations on the earth, according to His Word. Have you ever wondered why God blessed them? He told Abraham that He did this so that Israel could be a blessing to all the people. (Genesis 12:2) However, in the Old Testament we see how quickly they forgot this responsibility and how readily they sank into moral and spiritual decline. Then God sent prophets like Malachi, and there were seasons of revival. However, His people ultimately turned their backs on the One who made them a great nation. This pattern of obedience and disobedience, blessing and consequences, repeats itself throughout the Old Testament.

What can we learn from Israel that will help us as Americans avoid the destructive pattern we see in the Old Testament? In the next chapter I will share with you several key points of comparison with America and Israel that may open your eyes to the serious nature of the situation we are in today.

CHAPTER 6

Israel and America

Iᴛ's ᴀ sᴏɴɢ ᴍᴏsᴛ Aᴍᴇʀɪᴄᴀɴs ᴋɴᴏᴡ ʙʏ ʜᴇᴀʀᴛ. In 1918 Irving
Berlin, who also penned "White Christmas," wrote it. The Klu
Klux Klan rejected it because Berlin was a Jew. Kate Smith first
sang it on Armistice Day in 1938 as Hitler was gathering his Nazi
forces across the ocean. This iconic song then became a powerful
prayer that sustained our nation during World War II. The song? *God
Bless America.* However, it needs to be more than just a patriotic song;
it must continue to be a heartfelt prayer. We need to beg God again
to pour out His blessings on our nation. In fact, I am calling us to
focus on the 85th Psalm as a prayer to ask God to bless us again.

> You showed favor to your land, O LORD; you
> restored the fortunes of Jacob. You forgave the iniquity

of your people and covered all their sins. "Selah" You
set aside all your wrath and turned from your fierce
anger. Restore us again, O God our Savior, and put
away your displeasure toward us. Will you be angry
with us forever? Will you prolong your anger through
all generations? Will you not revive us again, that your
people may rejoice in you? Psalm 85:1-6

In the World Trade Organization (WTO), some nations are
designated as most-favored nations because they adhere to certain
standards and support human rights positions. In return, they are
allowed to trade freely with the other countries in the WTO. The
Bible teaches that there is a much more coveted status than being a
most-favored nation in the WTO – it is being a favored nation in
the eyes of God. The Bible says, "You showed favor to your land,
O Lord." (Psalm 85:1) The Psalmist was referring to Israel, but the
principle also holds true for America. Without a doubt, God has
shown His favor to our land in at least three ways.

God has blessed America materially

Compared to other nations, God has blessed us with abundant
natural resources. Thirty years ago we were dangerously dependent
on foreign oil. And we still import foreign oil, but in 2014 U.S. oil
production soared to its highest level since records were kept in 1900
with 8.7 million barrels of crude oil. In 2015, the U.S. passed Saudi
and Russia to become the leading oil producing nation in the world.

Most Americans are also wealthy compared to the rest of
the world. If you have more than one change of clothes, a roof
over your head and enjoy at least one hot meal per day, you are
richer than most of the earth's population. There are global wealth
calculators online that reveal where your income falls compared to
everyone else on the planet. For instance, if you make just $24,000
a year, you are wealthier than 92% of the world! If you make

$40,000 a year, you are wealthier than 96%. If you make $100,000 a year, you are in the top 1%. What are we doing with the resources God has poured out on America?

God has blessed us politically

I don't like politics. I like to say tongue-in-cheek that the word *politics* comes from two words: *poly* meaning "many" and *tics* meaning "blood-sucking pests." Someone has said that Columbus was the first American politician because he didn't know where he was going; when he got there, he didn't know where he was; and when he got back, he didn't know where he had been. And he did it all on someone else's money!

While I don't care for politicians, I cherish our political system. As we learned in an earlier chapter, America is a republic based upon the rule of law, and we vote to elect our leaders. Our Founding Fathers developed three branches of government to provide a system of checks and balances. While other nations around the world are fighting with different factions trying to take control, our nation has an orderly transfer of power from one president to the next.

However, John Adams noted a caveat to the safety and security of being in a republic. He once wrote in a letter, "Our constitution was made only for a religious and a moral people. It is wholly inadequate to the government of any other."[12] As more people turn away from faith in God, we may find ourselves more and more at the mercy of activist judges who rule based on their prejudices—rather than on the Constitution.

God has blessed us spiritually

Early explorers came to Central and South America in search of gold, but they came to North America in search of God. That is what makes our birth story as a nation unique among all the other nations on earth. Although modern media would disagree, a careful reading of history reveals that our Founding Fathers saw the formation of America as a spiritual task. John Quincy Adams wrote about this obligation to a friend: "The highest glory of the American Revolution was this: It connected in one indissoluble bond the principles of civil government with the precepts of Christianity."*13*

If you have had the opportunity to travel to other countries like China, for example, you know that religious freedom is a precious gift not to be taken for granted. Unlike many citizens around the world, we can attend the church of our choice—free from the fear of being arrested. During worship we don't have to look around to see if any government officials are spying on us. We can carry our Bibles openly and read God's Word. We can turn on a radio, TV or podcast to access the Word of God 24/7. These are privileges that many parts of the rest of the world do not have, but we take them for granted.

Our response to God's blessings has hurt us

We are also like the nation of Israel because we responded in the same way when God blessed us. God favored Israel, but they forgot the source of their blessings. I'm afraid America is likewise guilty of a short memory. The Founding Fathers wrote the opening paragraph of the Declaration of Independence to declare their belief in a Creator God who gives us our rights:

> "We hold these truths to be self-evident, [in other words, there is absolute truth] that all men are created equal [we exist because we are created by God], that they are endowed by the Creator with certain unalienable Rights [moral absolutes given to us by God], that among these are Life, Liberty and the pursuit of Happiness."

President Ronald Reagan explained the essential connection between God and society this way:

"Without God, there is no virtue, because there's no prompting of the conscience. Without God, we're mired in the material, that flat world that tells us only what the senses perceive. Without God, there is a coarsening of the society. And without God, democracy will not and cannot long endure. If we ever forget that we're one nation under God, then we will be a nation gone under."

–Dallas Ecumenical Prayer Breakfast, August 23, 1984

However, our modern culture has moved away from this "archaic" idea of a personal God. What are the signs and consequences of a nation that has forgotten God? The following two examples are at the top of the list.

1. We have reversed our values.

Times they are a changin'. Did you know that in 1965 26% of babies were born out of wedlock, but in 2015 about 41% were born out of wedlock? It's becoming the norm. The First Church of Cannabis opened its doors in Indiana in 2015, and the IRS approved their non-profit status. Sometimes I feel like crying out with the Psalmist: "Will you not revive us again, that your people may rejoice in you?" (Psalm 85:6)

I've heard it said, "You can't legislate morality." I disagree. Every piece of legislation reflects someone's morality. In their excellent book, *U-Turn: Restoring America to the Strength of Its Roots*, researcher George Barna and David Barton (founder of WallBuilders) give clear-cut evidence how our national values have made a U-turn from what we used to uphold as American values.[14] For example, they point out that our culture used to believe in truth and honesty. Now, truth is relative because "what's true for you may not be true for me." Back then, hard work was valued. Now, hand-outs are preferable. According to an article in *Forbes Magazine*, in 2011 about 49% of

Americans were receiving government benefits. With the addition of Obama Care, that number grew to 52% in just three years. The authors continue to contrast the value of civic duty versus prevalent civic unrest, the sanctity of family versus the total dismantling of the definition and on and on it goes.

2. We have removed God-talk from our public life.

For the first 20 decades of our history, God was an essential part of our national conversation. Our governmental leaders led more national calls to prayer than our church leaders did during the first few decades or our nation's history. Don't believe it? History records 1,020 calls to public prayer up until the year 1815. Our government issued almost 800 of these, with just 238 being issued by church leaders![15]

Since Ronald Reagan, U.S. presidents have been issuing a proclamation for the National Day of Prayer each May, and they have hosted corresponding prayer services in the White House. President Obama still issued the proclamation, but in 2009 he stopped hosting a prayer service at the White House. In East Texas where I live, people sometimes say we are in a bubble. That may be, but I think of it as a bubble of morality and sanity! I'm glad that many of our public events open with prayer. I prayed the invocation at an event at the University of Texas at Tyler recently. Prayer is offered at our public high school graduation ceremonies. Our city council meetings open with prayer. However, I realize that we are a remnant compared to the rest of our nation.

When the allied forces launched the D-Day invasion, President Franklin D. Roosevelt didn't just issue a proclamation that evening asking Americans to pray for our troops. In a national radio broadcast, he actually *led* our nation in prayer over the airwaves—an eloquent, fervent prayer that lasted over six minutes. As you read the following excerpt from his prayer in 1944, imagine a modern U.S. president leading the entire nation in similar fashion:

Almighty God,

Our sons, pride of our Nation, this day have set upon
a mighty endeavor, a struggle to preserve our Republic,
our religion, and our civilization, and to set free a
suffering humanity. They will need Thy blessings...
And, O Lord, give us Faith. Give us Faith in Thee...
With Thy blessing, we shall prevail over the unholy
forces of our enemy. Thy will be done, Almighty God.

Amen.

Wouldn't it be wonderful if God would give America a president
who would not just tell us to pray but also lead us in prayer?

The Washington Monument, whose construction began in 1848,
is the tallest structure in Washington, D.C. at 555 feet. By law, no
building can be constructed taller than this iconic symbol that was
originally dedicated in honor of George Washington. Do you know
what is inscribed at the pinnacle of the Washington Monument?
These words from scripture: *Laus Deo*, which is Latin for what the
Psalmist wrote: "Let God be praised." There may be legislators who
don't know that those words are heralded high above our capital city.
There may have been presidents who never knew that. There may be
Supreme Court justices who don't know that. However, no matter
how much our modern culture works to remove God-talk from the
public conversation, the invitation of our forefathers will always be,
"Let God be praised." We can still lift up our eyes and praise God for
the greatness and the blessings on this great land and beg God to once
again send His blessings on America.

Our survival depends on spiritual revival

Remember the pattern in the Old Testament? Israel turned from God
many times in their history, but there were also seasons of spiritual

renewal. This is one more example of our similarities. There have been three spiritual awakenings in America's history as well. I wrote a book years ago about the Ten Commandments called *Ten Requirements for America's Survival*. I truly believe we are only a prayer away from experiencing the kind of spiritual renewal in our country that can save us from the brink of disaster.

In every spiritual awakening, two important steps have led to revival: prayer and repentance. It works like this. Revival always begins with a heavy burden for spiritual renewal. The weight of that burden produces brokenness, and brokenness produces a fresh desire for prayer, which leads to repentance. If you long to be part of revival in our nation, you must understand the biblical principles that underline it.

First, let's talk about prayer's role in revival. The Third Great Awakening in America that began in 1857 is a fascinating illustration of how revival unfolds in a nation and changes the spiritual landscape almost overnight. In what became known as the Great Panic of 1857, the economy had nosedived, shutting down factories, sending railroads into bankruptcy and putting thousands of New Yorkers out of work. A quiet former businessman in New York City named Jeremiah Lanphier was elected by his church to serve as a lay missionary in the city, even though he had no prior experience. Joseph became burdened for the spiritual condition of his city and nation and announced he was going to host a noon prayer meeting once a week at his church. This is the invitation he posted:

> This meeting is intended to give merchants, mechanics, clerks, strangers, and business men generally an opportunity to stop and call upon God amid the perplexities incident to their respective avocations. It will continue for one hour; but it is also designed for those who may find it inconvenient to remain more than five or ten minutes, as well as for those who can spare the whole hour.[16]

The first day in September Jeremiah waited alone in the church in silence for half an hour before six people came to pray. The next week, there were 20 people. In two weeks, the small meeting had grown to 40 people and it was decided to start having daily prayer meetings. When another financial crash occurred suddenly in mid-October, closing the banks and leaving families to grow hungry, attendance at the prayer meetings grew to 3,000 almost instantaneously. Everyone from lawyers and physicians to merchants and messenger boys were driven to pray and seek God's face in the midst of this disaster. In six months, 10,000 New Yorkers were spending every noon hour in prayer. Shops posted signs that read, "Closed for Prayer." The movement then spread across the nation. In Chicago, over 3,000 people turned up to pray at the Metropolitan Theater. The same thing occurred over and over for months from coast to coast. Incredibly, over a million Americans became Christians during what came to be known as the Fulton Street Revival that lasted through 1860. It probably would have continued had the nation not been thrust into the Civil War. [17]

Is it possible for that to happen again? Today there are more mosques than churches in London. It wasn't always that way. In the early 20th century a spiritual awakening swept Britain, led by a simple coal miner named Evan Roberts in Wales. By his own account he attended church one evening and prayed this simple prayer, "God, bend me, break me!" In response, God broke his heart under a burden for His people. Roberts began traveling the countryside encouraging young people to gather together to pray and repent. Thousands soon filled the churches. The revival was so profound that the mules in coal mines had to be retrained because the miners stopped using profanity in their commands!

Notice that God did not use a preacher to lead these two examples of spiritual awakening. Prayer is always the catalyst for revival, but don't wait for your church or your preacher to lead you to do it. Will you ask God to break your heart and give you a burden for revival in America? You never know how God may use you.

Prayer is the first step in revival. The second step is repentance. God says in 2 Chronicles 7:14 that in addition to praying ("seeking His face"), God's people must "turn from their wicked ways." One of the best examples in the Bible of God getting the attention of an entire nation overnight is the story of King Josiah. The background on the story begins long after David and Solomon ruled a unified kingdom. The nation of Israel had split into the northern (Israel) and southern (Judah) kingdoms. Tragically, both kingdoms soon forgot about God. However, a boy named Josiah became king of Judah when he was only eight years old.

When he was a teenager, God changed his heart to seek after the God of David when some of his men made an unintended discovery one day. Josiah had ordered men to tackle some maintenance issues on the long-neglected temple. In doing so, they discovered a lost scroll containing God's Law. They hadn't consulted God's Word in several generations, so when the king blew the dust off the "Bible" and read God's Word for himself, he tore his clothes in anguish. Josiah commanded the people to restore the temple immediately and begin making animal sacrifices to the Lord once more. He also led the nation to renew the covenant and to celebrate Passover for the first time in many years. I love the message God gave to Josiah: "…'Because your heart was responsive and you humbled yourself before the Lord when you heard what I have spoken against this place and its people—that they would become a curse and be laid waste— and because you tore your robes and wept in my presence, I also have heard you,' declares the Lord." (2 Kings 22:19)

The nation of Israel experienced revival, but it would not have happened apart from heartfelt repentance. The same thing could happen in America if once again we would open His Book, blow the dust off and obey it.

Who can lead us to a new day in America?

As the rest of our nation shifts away from God, the Church will by necessity become more counter-cultural. Our positions on morality will become the minority, and the world will try to silence us. That's the way it has always been with God's people. In a culture war, we must stand for biblical morality. But we must do so with biblical grace. The Bible says in 1 Corinthians 13:1, "If I speak in the tongues of men and angels, and have not love, I'm nothing but a sounding brass or a tinkling cymbal." Victory is not about winning elections or court cases. It is about winning souls. We mustn't wring our hands at rulings that oppose biblical teaching. It's our opportunity to instead use them as a catalyst to mobilize a generation of pro-life and pro-marriage Christians who support biblical values.

After the last protest has long since ended and the U.S. Supreme Court is nothing but a tiny blip in history, Jesus Christ will continue to reign. Every person will stand before a living God to give an account for what he or she did with Jesus. Job One for the church is to lovingly spread the Good News that Jesus Christ can save anyone.

The greatest problem we face in America isn't the economy. It isn't abortion or the redefinition of marriage. Our biggest problem is sin. All the other problems are manifestations of the basic problem of every person—sin. The government doesn't have an answer for the sin problem, but the Bible does. His name is Jesus, and in the next chapter we will find out why we need Him in America now more than ever.

CHAPTER 7

America Needs a Shepherd

I T WAS A CHILLY 36 DEGREES AT CAPE CANAVERAL WHEN THE
SPACE SHUTTLE CHALLENGER LAUNCHED IN JANUARY 1986—15
DEGREES COLDER THAN ANY PREVIOUS SHUTTLE LAUNCH. Seventy-
six seconds after takeoff, a half-inch wide O-ring hardened by the
cold failed, causing the solid rocket booster to explode. All seven
crewmembers were killed. Investigations would later reveal that the
tragedy could have been prevented. Six months prior to the launch,
an engineer named Roger Boisjoly discovered that the O-rings would
harden and fail when subjected to low temperatures. He warned his
colleagues about "a catastrophe of the highest order" involving "loss
of human life" in what is now an infamous internal memo. However
the warning was ignored.

God sent prophets to do exactly what Boisjoly did—warn God's people that unless their behavior changed, disaster would follow. The books of the Minor Prophets, as they are called, are short in length. However, as we have seen, they contain many powerful insights into how God relates to individuals and to nations. The majority of these prophets spoke God's word of warning to Israel and Judah, but these warnings also addressed other nations as well. The prophet Micah preached 2,700 years ago, but his message contains timeless spiritual truths that still speak to our spiritual condition in America today.

Before God can heal us, our hearts must be broken

What strikes me about Micah's prophecy is the opening scene of a nation that has aroused God's anger. The Lord, he says, has had enough:

> The word of the LORD that came to Micah of Moresheth during the reigns of Jotham, Ahaz and Hezekiah, kings of Judah—the vision he saw concerning Samaria and Jerusalem.
>
> Hear, O peoples, all of you, listen, O earth and all who are in it, that the Sovereign LORD may witness against you, the Lord from his holy temple. Look! The LORD is coming from his dwelling place; he comes down and treads the high places of the earth. The mountains melt beneath him and the valleys split apart, like wax before the fire, like water rushing down a slope. All this is because of Jacob's transgression, because of the sins of the house of Israel. Micah 1:1-5

When the prophet describes the terrible judgment coming, poor Micah can hardly take it in. He is simply overcome with grief and finds himself wailing like a jackal and moaning like the loneliest owl in the darkest night. (Micah 1:1-9) If you've ever heard a pack of coyotes wailing, you know it's an eerie, unearthly noise. Can you imagine how it must have sounded for a human to utter a sound like that because of sheer heartbreak?

Until we feel the full weight of a sinful nation and until our hearts break with grief over what has happened to America, not much will change. Leonard Ravenhill was an evangelist from England who moved to the U.S. in the 1950s and retired to Garden Valley, Texas, before he died in 1994. If you have ever read his insightful writings, he seemed more like a 20ᵗʰ century prophet than a preacher. In 1979 he wrote about America's fatal flaws in a book called *America Is Too Young to Die*:

> Compared to the ancient civilizations, America was born only yesterday. But, and here is the rub, she is dying today and will be dead tomorrow unless there is a spiritual awakening...America can die, but it would have to be by suicide. It would be because she thinks God is dead, and because she believes that His laws, which, when broken, have felled every nation that ever lived, do not, in her hour of freedom and affluence, include her. America fights a battle that cannot be won at the ballot box. Her need is not the "new morality" of the hour, but the new morals based on the old laws of God.

Let's review the recurring pattern we've learned from the Old Testament. A nation is blessed. This leads to affluence and apathy. They then slide into immorality. God sends a warning that unless they repent, He will send judgment. If the nation turns to God, they are spared His punishment. If they ignore the message, the result is national disaster.

Where do you think America is right now in that pattern? Israel and Judah both ignored the warnings of the prophets for the last time, and their enemies consequently carried them into exile. Will America listen to the warnings, or will we ignore God's call for us to return to Him?

The evidence of immorality is mounting

I grew up watching Perry Mason, a television show about a sharp lawyer with a knack for coaxing criminals to confession. In fact, until I was seventeen years old and God called me to preach, I was planning on becoming a lawyer. At the most dramatic part of the show, Mason would typically introduce a crucial piece of evidence to sway the jury in favor of his client. Likewise, the prophet Micah employs courtroom language as he pictures God as a Mason-like prosecuting attorney presenting a case against Israel. God's judgment is not an arbitrary decision—it is always based on hard evidence. At this point in the book, I've already exposed several areas where we've gone off course as a nation. However, God's Word still has more to say. If we want to change where our country is headed, I think it's important to have a firm understanding of the full dimensions of the problem.

In Micah the Divine Prosecutor begins to outline specific and ample evidence regarding the moral decline of the nation. "Listen to what the Lord says: 'Stand up, plead your case before the mountains; let the hills hear what you have to say. Hear, O mountains, the Lord's accusation; listen, you everlasting foundations of the earth. For the Lord has a case against his people; he is lodging a charge against Israel.'" (Micah 6:1-2) God then presents the first of three sources of moral decline—the very trends we're seeing in America today.

1. Exhibit A: corrupt leadership

NBC Nightly News used to have a whistle blower segment entitled "The Fleecing of America." In it, they pointed out the high price Americans were paying regarding out of control government spending. Micah's message is so relevant to our governmental leaders today that they could have slipped it into the teleprompter at NBC during a Fleecing of America segment and no one would have noticed! God first addresses the leaders of a nation—the politicians, officials and others in positions of powerful influence over people.

He says:

> Listen, leaders of Jacob, leaders of Israel: Don't you
> know anything of justice? Haters of good, lovers of evil:
> Isn't justice in your job description? But you skin my
> people alive. You rip the meat off their bones. You break
> up the bones, chop the meat, and throw it in a pot for
> cannibal stew. The time's coming, though, when these
> same leaders will cry out for help to God, but he won't
> listen. He'll turn his face the other way because of their
> history of evil." Micah 3:1-4, *The Message*

There have always been corrupt politicians; they just haven't
always been caught. We've seen our share of them in America over the
past few years—whether it's a congressman using insider information
to beat the stock market, or a governor trying to sell a Senate seat to
the highest bidder.

In addition to corrupt politicians, other people in positions
of power have tried to alter the evidence in our history books and
classrooms to malign the true character, intentions and beliefs of our
Founding Fathers and make them sound "less religious." For example,
historians have tried to alter what we know about George Washington
in order to describe him as a Deist. In short, a Deist believes in an
impersonal God who isn't involved in His creation. However, one
of the earliest writings we have from Washington is an entry from
his personal prayer journal when he was twenty years old. They can
say what they want, but in this entry he sounds an awful lot like he's
praying to a personal God. Judge for yourself. Does this sound like a
non-committal prayer to a disinterested Deist?

> "O most glorious God ... remember that I am
> but dust and remit my transgressions, negligences,
> and ignorances, and cover them all with the absolute
> obedience of thy dear Son, through the sacrifice of
> Jesus Christ offered upon the cross for me ... wash

away my sin in the immaculate blood of the Lamb;
and purge my heart by thy Holy Spirit."[18]

Historian W. E. Woodward has even boldly asserted, "The name
of Jesus Christ is not mentioned even once in the vast collection of
Washington's published writings."[19] Is he correct? Absolutely not.
George Washington mentioned Jesus many times; his prayer journal
is full of powerful prayers calling on the grace and mercy of Christ.
What else are we to make of a letter (dated June 12, 1779) that
Washington wrote to a delegation of Delaware Native American
chiefs who inquired about educating their children in American
schools? Washington wrote: "You do well to wish to learn our arts
and ways of life, and above all, the religion of Jesus Christ. These will
make you a greater and happier people than you are. Congress will
do every thing they can to assist you in this wise intention."[20] Just
because it is said in a liberal classroom does not make it true; we must
become a student of history ourselves.

2. Exhibit B: cowardly pastors

I cannot overlook the fact that Micah brought the next powerful
indictment against a surprising culprit:

> Here is God's Message to the prophets, the
> preachers who lie to my people: "For as long as they're
> well paid and well fed, the prophets preach, 'Isn't life
> wonderful! Peace to all!' ... The sun has set on the
> prophets. They've had their day; from now on it's
> night. Visionaries will be confused, experts will be all
> mixed up. They'll hide behind their reputations and
> make lame excuses to cover up their God-ignorance."
> Micah 3:5, 7 *The Message*

America is in a moral mess, but I don't blame the corrupt
politicians; they've always existed. As Micah points out, much
of the true fault lies with the preachers—*we're* to blame for

letting our nation spiral out of control. We've been cowered into submission, thinking that if we said anything remotely political, the IRS would come get us. More than that, I believe many pastors have resisted speaking the hard truth because deep down we want people to like us. We don't want to say anything that might offend someone. Micah is right—we've been saying, "Life is wonderful...everything is fine!" Instead, we should have been the first ones sounding the alarm.

One of the leaders of the second Great Awakening in the 19th century was Charles Finney, a lawyer who later became an evangelist. It's been said that Finney could walk into a factory, lock eyes with the workers and under his steely gaze they would fall on their knees in repentance. (Just do a web search for an image of Finney—you might fall on your knees, too!) In one of his sermons entitled *The Decay of Conscience*, he had some harsh words for cowardly preachers:

> "If immorality prevails in the land, the fault is ours in a great degree. If there is a decay of conscience, the pulpit is responsible for it. If the church is degenerate and worldly, the pulpit is responsible for it. If Satan rules in our halls of legislation, the pulpit is responsible for it. If our politics become so corrupt that the very foundations of our government are ready to fall away, the pulpit is responsible for it. Let us not ignore this fact, my dear brethren; but let us lay it to heart, and be thoroughly awake to our responsibility in respect to the morals of this nation."

3. Exhibit C: complacent people

Dr. Elmer Peterson, the former Dean of the College of Education at Iowa State University, wrote an editorial that appeared in the *Daily Oklahoman* in 1951. In it he penned a scathing indictment against people who "want what they want" at any price:

> "A democracy cannot exist as a permanent form
> of government. It can only exist until the majority
> discovers it can vote itself largess [gifts of money] out
> of the public treasury. After that, the majority always
> votes for the candidate promising the most benefits
> with the result the democracy collapses because of the
> loose fiscal policy ensuing, always to be followed by a
> dictatorship, then a monarchy."

In Micah's time people paid money to hear exactly what they wanted to hear from their leaders. He wrote:

> Her leaders judge for a bribe, her priests teach for
> a price, and her prophets [translate godless politicians
> and preachers] tell fortunes for money. Yet they [the
> people] lean upon the Lord and say, "Is not the Lord
> among us? No disaster will come upon us." Therefore
> because of you, Zion will be plowed like a field,
> Jerusalem will become a heap of rubble, the temple hill
> a mound overgrown with thickets. Micah 3:11-12

Saying something is legally right doesn't mean it is morally right. Just because God delays His judgment does not mean it is not coming. Micah's fellow citizens had grown used to corruption…they even began to like it when it benefited them. Imagine their response when God one day essentially told them, "It's plowing time. Get ready. I've got my heavenly John Deere tractor revved up, and I'm headed your way with a row of 16-inch bottom plows."

There is hope for a nation in spiritual desperation

As is true with every message from God, there is also one more powerful promise of hope in Micah's message. Like Israel we're a nation of corrupt politicians, but not all of them are corrupt. We're also a nation of cowardly pastors, but some of us are changing that. And we're a nation of complacent people, but I challenge you to ask God to move you out of your apathy. The light that Micah saw on a future horizon was just a pinprick of hope that would take over 700 years to eventually grow into the brilliant glow of a million suns. He put what he saw in words, although he could not even put a name with the face of the coming ruler:

> But you, Bethlehem Ephrathah, though you are
> small among the clans of Judah, out of you will come
> for me one who will be ruler over Israel, whose origins
> are from of old, from ancient times...He will stand
> and shepherd his flock in the strength of the Lord,
> in the majesty of the name of the Lord his God. And
> they will live securely, for then his greatness will reach
> to the ends of the earth. And he will be their peace.
> Micah 5:2, 4-5

Who is Micah describing? He did not yet know His name, but Micah saw a Savior was going to be born in Bethlehem 730 years before it happened. Of course, we know now that the Shepherd Micah prophesied was Jesus. In fact, when the Magi came looking for the one who was born King of the Jews, the scholars of Herod the Great used this very prophecy to direct them to Bethlehem where Jesus was born!

Jesus wouldn't be just any shepherd, Micah said. This Shepherd's origins stemmed from ancient times, literally from everlasting ages ago. Even though this Shepherd would be born in a little obscure village, His worldwide impact would be immeasurable. What Micah said this Shepherd would accomplish are the same things we also desperately need Him to do in America today.

We need a Shepherd to give us guidance

Isaiah wrote, "We all, like sheep, have gone astray, each of us has turned to his own way; and the Lord has laid on Him the iniquity of us all." (Isaiah 53:6) Sheep are not intelligent animals. They're cute. They look sweet. However, you'll never see trained sheep in the circus and with good reason! America is a nation full of sheep—we cannot depend on our own intelligence to get our nation out of the mess we are in. We must look to the Shepherd for guidance since we do not know how to rescue ourselves.

We need a Shepherd to give us security

We have Social Security, but it doesn't seem very secure right now. We have a Department of Homeland Security, and even a National Security Agency, but most Americans feel insecure. Why is that? I believe the breakdown of the family has contributed to our general sense of instability. Everyone needs a place where they are safe, loved and accepted—a place where they learn the skills they need to navigate through life. That place is the family, but unfortunately there are fewer stable, God-centered families. Listen to Micah's description of fractured families and see if it doesn't reflect our American culture:

> For a son dishonors his father, a daughter rises
> up against her mother, a daughter-in-law against her
> mother-in-law—a man's enemies are the members of
> his own household. But as for me, I watch in hope for
> the Lord, I wait for God my Savior. Micah 7:6-7

Micah observed that part of Israel's greater problem could be traced to the individual breakdown of families. The family is the basic building block of a society; when families fail, an entire culture crumbles with it.

However, Micah says that the nation with God's Shepherd (Jesus) will "live securely." (5:5) If you've ever seen sheep grazing in an open field, you've probably noticed that they are not skittishly looking about for danger on the horizon. That's the shepherd's job. They're not worried about where their next meal is coming from. That's the shepherd's job. A shepherd's job is to keep the flock together—safe and secure—at all costs. The Christ-centered family can withstand the perils of raising children in today's modern culture and provide a safe place to nurture them in the admonition of the Lord. (Ephesians 6:4)

We need a Shepherd to give us peace

Micah points out another interesting characteristic of the Shepherd in 5:5. He says this Shepherd "will be their peace." Notice that he doesn't say the Shepherd will *bring* peace—He Himself will *be* their peace. When he receives this beautiful promise from God, Micah responds with astonishment...he can hardly believe the grace of God:

> Who is a God like you, who pardons sin and forgives the transgression of the remnant of his inheritance? You do not stay angry forever but delight to show mercy. You will again have compassion on us; you will tread our sins underfoot and hurl all our iniquities into the depths of the sea. Micah 7:18-19

The deepest valley in the ocean is deeper than the highest mountain on earth. Mt. Everest soars 29,000 feet, but the Mariana Trench in the Pacific Ocean drops to 36,000 feet below sea level. When you place your faith in Jesus, that's where God puts the guilt and shame of all of your sins. I love the fact that the Bible says that God "hurls" them into the depths of the sea—He doesn't just drop them overboard like a heavy anchor. He throws them far away into the depths of the sea, and then He posts a "No Fishing" sign. You've probably seen the bumper sticker that says: "No God. No peace. Know God. Know peace." If you know the Shepherd, His love and forgiveness can foster an incredible sense of personal peace that will uphold you even during the most turbulent times.

In the future, we may continue to see more so-called blue states and red states. We are a divided nation today, and that rift may deepen in future elections. However, those of us who follow Jesus already have a King. His name is King Jesus and He's not up for re-election! One day soon this King will return, and He won't be riding on a Democratic donkey or a Republican elephant. Revelation 19 says He'll be riding on a white horse and on His robe and on His thigh will be written the matchless title: "King of Kings and Lord of Lords!"

Are you worried about the future?

Even though we have Christ as our Shepherd, it's human nature to feel a gnawing sense of dread when the news paints a frightening picture of our future. We know Jesus will one day make everything right—but what should we do in the here and now? I'm trusting God for a spiritual awakening. However, if our nation does not return to God, it faces a scary future. It wasn't too long ago that the news media told us we're edging toward a "fiscal cliff." But I also think we're teetering on the edge of a moral and spiritual cliff as well. What's going to happen? There are plenty of people who are fearful about the future of our nation. However, as we'll see in the next chapter, God's Word tells us exactly what to do whenever we feel hopeless.

CHAPTER 8

Are You Worried about America's Future ?

I'M CERTAINLY NOT A PROPHET, BUT WHAT IF I TOLD YOU THAT EARLY NEXT YEAR WE WOULD SEE AN ECONOMIC IMPLOSION AND THE DOW WOULD DROP OVERNIGHT TO 100 POINTS? With our economy in ruins, a massive cyber-attack would then completely cripple the Internet, including our military defense system. A day later radical Muslims who have infiltrated our neighborhoods over the past 10 years would launch a coordinated attack across our nation. At midnight of that same day, Iran would launch a nuclear attack against Israel and the United States, destroying our military command and control centers—followed by a massive invasion of ISIS who would take control of our crippled nation. Americans who weren't immediately killed would be deported to Muslim countries to become slaves.

How would you react to a prediction like that?

Assuming you are still reading and haven't slammed this book shut, my guess is that you probably don't want me to even suggest something like that! Now you know why people hated most of the prophets—they hated their message. Habakkuk issued a doomsday prophecy very similar to what I have described about 20 short years before it happened when a powerful nation called Babylon pounced on the unsuspecting southern kingdom of Judah.

Other prophets had already warned them about this impending event. Maybe if Judah had listened then, things would have been different. However, from Habakkuk's perspective, God's judgment is now inevitable. There is no way they could be spared. His prophecy is different from every other minor prophet book because he doesn't preach to people—it's too late for that. The time for warning has passed and judgment is at the door.

Instead of a sermon, this book records a dialogue between Habakkuk and God, and we get to listen in. God informed Habakkuk that something so unexpected—and so awful—would soon happen that he wouldn't believe it even if he were told. To Habakkuk's surprise, God planned to use a pagan, godless nation as the instrument of His judgment against his own people.

What happened to Israel can happen to us

Today the nation of Israel is tiny, but it is strong. It is about the size of New Jersey, and its much larger enemies surround it. If we could rewind the clock 3,000 years when Israel was a leading world power with extensive borders, the contrast would be shocking. Under King Solomon the enormous size and extravagant wealth of the nation was at its peak.

When the Queen of Sheba (who ruled an impressive Egyptian kingdom herself) visited Solomon, she admitted she was overwhelmed by the wealth and influence of the sprawling Hebrew nation. (1 Kings 10:7) After several generations, however, Israel's influence and status in the world weakened as their moral and spiritual foundation eroded. In other words, without God, the nation floundered. In 587 B.C. the Babylonians captured the southern kingdom of Judah, including the once glorious city of Jerusalem. Ancient Babylon was located exactly where Iraq and Iran are today. It must have been devastating for the Jews to see the Babylonians destroy the beautiful temple that Solomon had built and then carry off the entire temple treasury. As a final blow to their morale, Babylon skimmed off and deported some of their best and brightest young men, including Daniel and his friends Shadrach, Meshach and Abednego.

This story from the Bible poses a sobering question for us to consider. If something like that could happen to God's chosen people, why should we expect God to treat America any differently?

Alexis de Tocqueville was a French historian who visited America in the 1800s to work on an academic study of American democracy. His massive work is entitled, *Democracy in America*. In President Eisenhower's speech on November 3, 1952, he quoted de Tocqueville as saying:

> I sought for the greatness of America in her
> harbors and rivers and fertile fields, and her mines and
> commerce. It was not there. Not until I went into the
> churches and heard her pulpits flame with righteousness
> did I understand the greatness of her power. America is
> great because she is good; and if America ever ceases to
> be good, America will cease to be great.

Remember, God blessed Israel so that they could be a blessing to other nations by their righteous example—a city set high on a hill. For so long America has been that same source of blessing and shining example to other nations. What now? Habakkuk asked God the same question. In fact, Habakkuk's name means, "to wrestle." He wrestled with God about what was going to happen next in light of present conditions.

God can handle your tough questions

This tiny book in the Bible has a powerful message to us as both Americans and as followers of Jesus. First, Habakkuk teaches us that we can ask God anything in prayer. (However, we may not always like His answers!)

Before God informed him that He was about to judge Judah, Habakkuk opened up the conversation by asking God a series of questions about why He wasn't doing anything about the growing immorality. He asked:

> How long, O Lord, must I call for help, but you
> do not listen? Or cry out to you, "Violence!" but you
> do not save? Why do you make me look at injustice?
> Why do you tolerate wrong? Destruction and violence
> are before me; there is strife, and conflict abounds.
> Therefore the law is paralyzed and justice never
> prevails. The wicked hem in the righteous so that
> justice is perverted. Habakkuk 1:1-6.

Have you ever asked God similar questions? Why doesn't He step in and right the wrongs in our nation today? Some people think it is blasphemy to question God. They are afraid to ask God, "What in the world are you doing? Why are all these bad things happening?" I suppose they think God will thunder back from heaven, "Don't ask me questions like that! Who are you to question my authority?" However, there's nothing wrong with asking God the tough questions. He can handle it. Just don't expect Him to give you the kind of answer you think you want to hear.

Job, another Old Testament character who suffered, questioned God. But he didn't get the answers he was looking for either. God started asking Job a lot of tough questions instead! Finally Job had to admit he wasn't wise enough to solve life's biggest problems. However, his trust was so strong that he promised to put his hope in God even if it killed him!

What bothers you about life, but you're afraid to ask? Maybe you want to know, "God, why is there cancer?" Or "God, why are there earthquakes and tornados?" Or "God, why does a madman kill innocent people?" Maybe the toughest questions you wrestle with address more personal issues. You may want to know why you and your mate cannot have children or why your elderly parents have to deal with so much physical pain. God isn't insulted by your questions. The root of the word "question" is not negative or subversive at all—it comes from the word "quest." We're all on a quest to try to understand life and understand God. I once saw in a dirt-floored Ugandan classroom a handwritten motto on the wall that said, "When I ask, I become a fool for a minute. But when I don't ask, I become a fool forever."

We ask, "Why?" but God often answers, "Watch"

In reply to his concerns over why the guilty went unpunished, God told Habakkuk: "Look at the nations and **watch**—and be utterly amazed. For I am going to do something in your days that you would not believe, even if you were told." (1:5) In other words, if Habakkuk could just wait for God to unveil His plan, he would have all the answers he needed.

We know it's okay to question God because there is a perfect example of this in the life of Jesus. John the Baptist was the forerunner of Jesus and had faithfully announced His coming. When he finally saw Him in the flesh, he pointed to Jesus and confidently asserted, "Look! The Lamb of God who takes away the sin of the world!" (John 1:36)

However, John later found himself battling serious doubts after he was thrown in prison for preaching about God. He even sent a messenger to Jesus to ask Him if He really was the Messiah after all. (Luke 7:20) Translation: "If you're the Messiah, then what am I doing here in prison?" Jesus didn't criticize John for his pointed question. He didn't give him a trite answer either. Instead, Jesus told the messenger to tell John the same thing God told Habakkuk—"Look and watch." Jesus pointed to the miraculous evidence that God was at work through Him—healing the lame and helping the blind to see. The implied answer to John's implied question was, "Of course I'm the Messiah. See what I'm doing...and what I will do for you, too."

Whenever you are at a confusing place in your life and you want to ask God why things are happening the way they are, look around. What do you see? Where do you see the undeniable activity of God? We most often want to ask, "Why?" when a better question in times of pain and confusion is, "What?" Ask God, "What are you trying to show me?" I love the attitude of Ruth Bell Graham who once wrote: "I lay my 'whys?' before Your cross in worship kneeling; my mind too numb for thought, my heart beyond all feeling. And worshipping, I realize that in knowing You I don't need a 'why.'"

We live by God's promises, not His explanations

God is under no obligation to explain to us why He does or doesn't act in a certain manner.

> "For my thoughts are not your thoughts, neither are your ways my ways," declares the LORD. "As the heavens are higher than the earth, so are my ways higher than your ways and my thoughts than your thoughts." Isaiah 55:8-9

We live in the information age where we can Google anything that comes to our mind and receive an almost instantaneous answer.

Therefore, we've come to prefer explanations in short order to whatever vexes us. In contrast, the Bible promises peace without having to know all the answers. Jesus said, "Peace I leave with you; my peace I give you. I do not give to you as the world gives. Do not let your hearts be troubled and do not be afraid." (John 14:27) The kind of peace that Jesus gives does not depend on receiving information about why God does what He does. The Bible says that His peace is something that far surpasses our need to understand the facts. Besides, sometimes the facts just don't make sense, do they? For example, even if God allowed us to "understand" why someone we loved died too soon, it probably would not make us feel better. When we do not understand what God is doing, He gives us the incredible promise that we can find peace because "...the peace of God, *which transcends all understanding*, will guard your hearts and your minds in Christ Jesus." (Philippians 4:7)

It's okay to question God, but when your questions go largely unanswered, just trust Him instead. On the cross Jesus asked, "My God, my God, WHY have you forsaken me?" However, in the final moments before Jesus died, He entrusted His spirit—and His questions—to God. (Matthew 27:46)

In the final part of their dialogue, Habakkuk also came to a place where he didn't seek any more answers about why God allowed the moral fabric of the country to unravel. Instead he just stood in awe of the majesty of God. He said, "Lord, I have heard of your fame; I stand in awe of your deeds, O Lord. Renew them in our day, in our time make them known; in wrath remember mercy." (Habakkuk 3:2) That should be our prayer for our nation during these days. Instead of being consumed by worry, we should pray in faith that God will have mercy.

Learn to move from worry to worship in uncertain times

Sometimes after you read or listen to the news about the escalating violence in our nation and in our world, you may find yourself consumed with worry and fear. That's a natural reaction. That was also Habakkuk's first response when he realized just how much trouble his nation was in! He wrote, "I heard and my heart pounded, my lips quivered at the sound; decay crept into my bones, and my legs trembled." (Habakkuk 3:16) He correctly describes the physical symptoms of apprehension—uncontrollable trembling, a rapid heart rate, etc. Worry and fear can make you physically ill! Inscribed on the Jefferson Memorial are these fateful words: "I tremble for my country when I think that God is just; that his justice cannot sleep forever."

However, Habakkuk introduces a great theme that is repeated three times in the New Testament when he says, "The righteous will live by his faith." (Habakkuk 2:4) It is easy to live by fear—that comes naturally. But we can live by faith instead. Habakkuk's prophecy begins with, "Oh, no! Things are awful!" Yet he ends his message with the assurance, "Oh, right! God's in control!"

While some American Christians are moaning and groaning about "how bad it is for us" in a liberal society, we could all benefit from a quick reality check. We have Christian brothers and sisters around the world being beheaded for their faith and we're upset about a Supreme Court ruling? It seems petty for American churches to worry about losing their tax-exempt status after I read about the teenage Muslim girl who became a Christian and refused to recant Christ even while her father broke every bone in her hand as punishment. We're not suffering. The Gospel is thriving around the world in the face of persecution. Even if we lose a few cultural battles, in the end, we know who wins the war!

Will you rejoice in the Lord even in bad times?

Habakkuk's world was crumbling, and his nation was facing annihilation. Even so, he makes one of the most powerful professions of faith in the Bible:

> Though the fig tree does not bud and there are
> no grapes on the vines, though the olive crop fails

and the fields produce no food, though there are no sheep in the pen and no cattle in the stalls, yet I will rejoice in the Lord, I will be joyful in God my Savior. Habakkuk 3:17-18

The word that Habakkuk uses in this passage for *Savior* is *Yeshua*, which means *Jesus*. The word he uses for *rejoice* literally means "to spin around and dance for joy." That's what faith does in the face of fear! It takes zero faith to sing and rejoice when everything is going great in your life. But when life has bottomed out, it requires all the faith you can muster to dance a jig before God.

Here is my 21st century paraphrase of what this passage in Habakkuk means:

> Though my taxes keep going up, though my savings are depleted and my investments are shrinking, though my candidate didn't win and I'm scared about our future, though I got a bad report from the doctor and I hurt all over, though my friends have deserted me and I feel all alone, though life seems unfair and I feel mistreated...YET I will jump for joy in the Lord! I will spin around and sing for delight in my God who is Jesus!"

Notice Habakkuk wasn't rejoicing in his crop failure. He was rejoicing in God's love for him *despite everything*. He didn't just say he was rejoicing in THE Lord; he was rejoicing in "*my* God." What is the difference? Martin Luther said that good theology is a matter of pronouns. It's one thing to say, "That's a cool car!" And it's another thing to say, "That's MY car!" It's one thing to say, "Jesus is the Lord." It's another thing to say, "Jesus is MY Lord!" Sure, there are many things happening in our world today that try to rob our joy and cause us to be anxious. However, the Bible says, "Cast all your anxiety on him because he cares for you." (1 Peter 5:7)

Bob was known as a consummate worrier. He worried about anything and everything. He not only worried about his problems—he worried about problems of other people, too. He took worrying to an art form. But one day Bob showed up for work with a smile on his face, shoulders back and with a spring in his step. His coworkers soon noticed the change in his disposition, and one of them said, "You don't seem worried today! What happened?"

Bob answered, "The greatest thing happened. I hired a guy full-time to worry for me. I tell him what's wrong and he worries about it, so I don't have to!"

"That's a great idea! How much are you paying him?"

"I pay him $100,000 a year."

At this, his friend said, "But, Bob, you don't make that much money in a year! How are you going to pay him?"

Bob just smiled and replied, "I don't know, but that's his worry, not mine!"

Wouldn't it be great if you had someone you could tell your problems to, and then you wouldn't have to worry anymore? You do have someone like that. His name is Jesus. If you are struggling with worry, go ahead and write your own paraphrase of Habakkuk 3:17-18. Make a list of all the things that are going wrong in your life, and then look to heaven and say, "YET I will rejoice in God MY Savior!"

Follow Jesus one step at a time

Every year when I take a group of church members to visit Israel, we visit the Dead Sea. On our way down there from Jerusalem, the Dead Sea is on the left and the rugged Judean hills rise steeply on the right side. These crags and mountains have changed little since David played hide-and-seek with Saul in them 3,000 years ago. In fact, they've changed little in the 2,000 years since Jesus spent 40 days there praying and fasting. As our tour bus ambles along, our tour guide named Reuven usually promises a soda to the first passenger who can spot a biblical animal called an ibex. The mountains are full of these small deer with long, thin horns.

This is the animal Habakkuk had in mind in his final verse. He wrote, "The Sovereign Lord is my strength; he makes my feet like the feet of a deer, he enables me to go on the heights." (Habakkuk 3:19) How do the ibex walk with confidence on the treacherous mountain crags? Why don't they slip and fall, particularly when they can't even see their hind feet? Simple. Animals like the ibex, including mountain goats, walk in an unusual way. They put their front feet on secure ground and, through instinct or conditioning, their back feet always step in exactly the same spot where their front feet just stepped.

We don't have four feet; we have only two—and some of us have two left feet! How will we make it through a narrow mountain trail of trouble and adversity in life? How can we make sure we don't fall from the heights? Just step in the footprints of our Lord who is going before us. He never asks us to go anywhere where His feet have not already walked. "Christ suffered for you, leaving you an example, *that you should follow in his steps.*" (1 Peter 2:21) As we face a scary future, don't be afraid. Just keep following the footsteps of Jesus.

What can we do about it?

I often say that if you cannot do anything about a situation, don't worry about it. However, if there is something you can do about it, do it! As I look around at the demise of our American culture, I am heartsick. I trust that you are too or you would not be reading this book. Many concerned Christians are asking the same question, "What can we do?"

This is a question David raised in the Psalms. Bible scholars believe that David wrote the 11th Psalm before he was king and he was living in the courts of Saul (the first king of Israel). Under a disobedient, jealous leader like Saul, the people had become very rebellious and indifferent toward God. David was appalled by the moral and spiritual decline of a nation that had been steeped in godly heritage. He asked the question, "When the foundations are being destroyed, what can the righteous do?" (Psalm 11:3) What can you do about our nation as an average citizen? What is your responsibility before God? I'm glad you asked! But be sure you know what you're asking. In fact, my advice is that you don't read this final chapter unless you are willing to apply what you discover. Turns out, God's Word has very specific instructions for Christians when our moral, historical and spiritual foundations are crumbling all around us.

CHAPTER 9

Lord,
Heal Our Land

I BELIEVE THAT IF OUR FOUNDING FATHERS COULD COME BACK FROM THE DEAD AND VISIT AMERICA TODAY, THEY WOULD NOT RECOGNIZE IT. For example, I believe the current size of the federal government would shock them. From my study of history and the writings of many of our forefathers, I believe their original intent was to give the various states more rights and to limit the size of the federal government. In 1824 Thomas Jefferson wrote in a letter two short years before he died about what he considered to be the alarming size of the government at that time: "I think, myself, that we have more machinery of government than is necessary, too many parasites living on the labor of the industrious." What do you think his reaction would be to the news that in 2015 that there were about 2.5 million federal employees? In 1824 federal spending was about 2% of our GNP; in 2015 it was over 25%!

Why have we changed so much in such a short time? I believe it has to do with the threats to the very bedrock of our nation— specifically our damaged moral, historical and spiritual foundations that can no longer support the weight of a nation that has lost its way. But what can we do about it?

We must speak the truth in love

First, when we see that our moral foundations are being dismantled, we must be willing to speak the truth and do so in love. In 1987, ABC news commentator Ted Koppel said something in a commencement speech at Duke University that might get him fired if he dared speak something similar today:

> Our society finds truth too strong a medicine to digest undiluted. In its purest form, truth is not a polite tap on the shoulder; it is a howling reproach. When Moses walked down from Mt. Sinai, he brought the Ten Commandments, not the Ten Suggestions.

It's never popular to speak the truth in a wayward culture, and it's become even more unpopular to do so in recent years. Yet it was not always this way. I've visited the United States Supreme Court building several times and have often thought how many U.S. citizens might be surprised to learn that a statue of Moses appears twice, holding the Ten Commandments. On a third statue picturing Justice, there are 10 Roman numerals. Up until 1988, the official guidebook of the building noted that these 10 numbers represented the Ten Commandments. However, today if you're given a tour, you may be told that those 10 numbers represent the Ten Amendments to the Constitution!

I have made a deliberate attempt to re-print as much evidence of our forefathers' commitment to Christian values as I can within these few chapters. I want to leave no doubt that our Founding Fathers upheld the importance of a strong Christian foundation for America.

Noah Webster is but one more example—and his topic of choice is the educational system. Webster, one of our Founding Fathers who has been called the Schoolmaster of the Republic, wrote in 1828:

> In my view, the Christian religion is the *most important and one of the first things* in which *all* children, under a free government, ought to be instructed. No truth is more evident to my mind than that the Christian religion must be the basis of any government intended to secure the rights and privileges of a free people.

For most of our nation's history, we have recognized the moral foundation of the Bible, but that is no longer the case. There is no longer a moral majority in America. Those who believe the Bible are instead a shrinking minority. However, don't be alarmed by that fact; from the beginning of our faith, Christians were always the underdogs. First Century Christians lived in a pagan, sex-crazed Roman culture that was far worse than anything we experience in America today. Paul wrote an admonition to the moral minority during that time, and it still applies to us:

> For it is God who works in you to will and to act according to his good purpose. Do everything without complaining or arguing, so that you may become blameless and pure, children of God without fault in a crooked and depraved generation, in which you shine like stars in the universe as you hold out the word of life. Philippians 2:13-16

Whenever a ruling or an elected official departs from America's traditional biblical morals, our natural, human reaction is to do the two things the Bible says NOT to do—complain and argue. For example, after the 2015 Supreme Court ruling on gay marriage, many Christians voiced their complaints to supporters in an argumentative, unloving tone. Instead, the Bible says that we need to keep letting our light shine in a crooked and depraved culture.

After the fall of the Roman Empire, Europe entered a time the historians call the Dark Ages. Morally speaking, America is now entering the darkest period of her history, which is why we so desperately need to uphold the light of truth. We will never forsake the truth of God's Word, but we must speak it in love. I'm not going to argue with anyone who disagrees with my beliefs. But I'm happy to enter into a respectful conversation with anyone about what the Bible says about morality. Study the issues and let your voice be heard. We may be a minority, but we cannot afford to be a silent minority. Use every means necessary—social media, letters to the editor, letters to government leaders, etc. But don't be angry or argue your point. Demonstrate the love of Christ in everything you say and do.

I mentioned in an earlier chapter that President George Washington's first act as president was to pray for God's blessings on our nation. In that same inaugural speech on April 30, 1789, he did not hesitate to describe the conditions that would necessitate God's removing His blessings from our nation: "The propitious *(favorable)* smiles of Heaven can never be expected on a nation that disregards the eternal rules of order and right, which Heaven itself has ordained." In other words, while God has smiled on our nation, our first president solemnly warned that if our nation ever departs from God's laws, the natural consequence is that His smile would turn to a frown. Do you think God is smiling or frowning on our nation right now? Our moral foundation that has supported this nation for centuries is now in jeopardy of collapsing, but that's not all. Our historical foundations are also under attack.

We must teach a new generation the truth

Second, when we find our historical foundations are at risk, we must teach a new generation the truth. In this book, I've cited the intentional efforts by some secular educators to revise our history in order to remove or blur any references to God, Jesus or the Bible. If you recall the quote of Noah Webster, he believed that Christianity is the basis of all public education. Up until the last half of the 20th century, all schools in America could be considered Christian schools because teachers read from the Bible and led students in prayer.

In sounding the alarm, I want to include some final specific examples of how our historical foundation of Christian faith has been revised. Consider the traditional story of the first Thanksgiving. As we know, the Pilgrims landed in 1620 in what is now Massachusetts. Unprepared to face the harsh brutality of a New England winter, many of them died before spring arrived. With the help of neighboring Native Americans, they then successfully planted more crops and reaped a harvest to sustain them in their second winter. In 1621, together with these new neighbors, they held a feast of thanksgiving to God for His blessings.

This is the story our children are hearing in public schools today, right? Not necessarily. In a study conducted by a New York University professor of psychology of 1st-6th grade textbooks, much of the information devoted to the Pilgrims neglected to mention their religious faith.[21] "Pilgrim" was defined as "someone who travels a long distance," and the depiction of Thanksgiving presented the Pilgrims and Native Americans *thanking each other* for their help in surviving the harsh conditions. Curiously, giving thanks to God was not mentioned.

Historian Kenneth C. Davis, author of the popular series *Don't Know Much About History*, glosses over the religious heritage of our nation. For example, he mentions the Mayflower Compact, but he conveniently omits the parts of the document that mention God or the Christian faith. His quote of the Mayflower Compact is below (the parts he omitted are underlined): [22]

"Having undertaken, <u>for the Glory of God, and advancements of the Christian faith and honor of our King and Country</u>, a voyage to plant the first colony in the Northern parts of Virginia, do by these presents, solemnly and mutually, <u>in the presence of God, and one another</u>, covenant and combine ourselves together into a civil body politic."

In the same book, Davis quotes the famous speech by Patrick Henry, but notice what parts he leaves out from Henry's complete speech (omissions underlined):[23]

"<u>An appeal to arms and to the God of hosts is all that is left us. We shall not fight alone. God presides over the destinies of nations, and will raise up friends for us. The battle is not to the strong alone; it is to the vigilant, the active, the brave.</u> Is life so dear, or peace so sweet as to be purchased at the price of chains of slavery? <u>Forbid it, Almighty God!</u> I know not what course others may take, but as for me, give me liberty or give me death!"

The result of these efforts to reposition and rewrite history to suit a politically correct culture has created a generation of children with little to no exposure to the powerful spiritual influence of our Founding Fathers. We need to teach our children and young adults that America's history is full of references to their dependence on God, Jesus and the Bible.

I'm not blaming the schools. The primary place children should be learning about the Bible and truth is not in the schoolroom but in the home. As Moses was preparing to take a new generation into the Promised Land, he gave this assignment to the parents:

Only be careful, and watch yourselves closely so that you do not forget the things your eyes have seen or let them slip from your heart as long as you live. Teach them to your children and to their children after them. Deuteronomy 4:9

I thank God for every home-school family and every Christian school in America that are teaching biblical and historical truth to the students. But we can't give up on public schools. I am grateful for every teacher, administrator and student who attends public school and sees it as a mission field to let his or her light shine for Jesus. Of course, another way to teach a new generation is to lead by example and register to vote and vote according to your convictions. What does it say to young people if we have given up hope in the democratic process? Heaven hears our prayers, but Washington counts our votes. I've addressed the collapse of our moral and historical foundations. However, another foundation is under attack—and its demise, above all others, should move us to take action.

We must cry out in desperation to God

Third, when our spiritual foundations are removed, God's people must cry out to Him. God's solution for every rebellious nation is recorded in 2 Chronicles 7:14, which He presented to the people attending Solomon's dedication ceremony for the beautiful new temple. God explained, "If my people, who are called by my name will humble themselves and pray and turn from their wicked ways, then will I hear from heaven and will forgive their sin and will heal their land." Most Christians know that verse by heart. However, verse 19 warns what will happen if God's people forsake Him and His ways. He essentially says, "I'll uproot you from this land. I'll reject this temple, and I will make you a laughing stock among the other nations." Israel eventually made the wrong choice in this heavenly ultimatum by disobeying God. America now faces the same choice.

It is disheartening to see many Christians in America lashing out in anger about the direction of our nation. That is not the response

God describes in 2 Chronicles. The example of the prophets we've studied in this book—and the example of Jesus Himself—is to be so burdened by sin that we fall on our knees and our eyes fill with tears. Jesus stood on the Mount of Olives and wept bitter tears over the spiritual condition of Jerusalem. The prophet Jeremiah was called the "weeping prophet" because he cried over the spiritual condition of Judah. An entire book in the Bible contains Jeremiah's tear-stained prayers—it's called Lamentations. I challenge you to read through it and substitute the name *America* for every reference to Israel in order to inspire you to pray.

However, in the midst of his darkness, Jeremiah also saw hope shining like a bright star. He prayed:

> I remember my affliction, the bitterness and the gall, and my soul is downcast within me. *Yet this I call to mind and therefore I have hope*: Because of the LORD's great love we are not consumed, for his compassions never fail. They are new every morning; great is your faithfulness. Lamentations 3:19-23

We have to have hope going forward in the promise of God's Word. He can heal our land again.

The most important action to take

What can the righteous do when the moral, historical and spiritual foundations are falling apart all around us? We must speak the truth in love, teach a new generation the truth and cry out in desperation to God. However, some may not like what I've saved for last in answer to that question.

In a culture war of convictions, it's possible to disagree without being disrespectful. We want to say "we" are right and "they" are wrong. But we must be careful that we don't become conceited and think that we are any *better* than those with whom we disagree. The moment you start feeling superior to anyone who disagrees with you, then you have become like a Pharisee. In the time of Jesus, these religious leaders believed they were the good guys and everyone else, including Jesus, were bad guys.

What makes a good guy good? The Bible answers this question unequivocally in Romans 3:10 by explaining there is "no one righteous, not even one..." The only righteousness we have is what God has imparted to us. The Bible says it this way: "God made him who had no sin to be sin for us, so that in him we might become the righteousness of God." (2 Corinthians 5:21) When you surrender your self-righteousness and admit that you are a sinner, then you come to a place where God can give you the righteousness of Jesus. When you stand in the righteousness of Jesus, it's not your goodness that counts; it's HIS righteousness.

Finally, the most important action you can take as a concerned Christian is to pray! Pray as you have never prayed before for our nation. There is great power when people pray together. This doesn't mean that we have to be in the same physical location. However, we can pray at the same time for the same thing. Based on 2 Chronicles 7:14 I'm asking everyone who reads this book to join me in praying every day at 7:14 for God to restore America. It can be 7:14 am or 7:14 pm, or both. Set your smart phone or an alarm clock, and start praying. Let's bombard heaven with our prayers for God to restore America and heal our land.

Lord, Heal Our Land ★ A Call to Prayer for America

ENDNOTES

1 John Winthrop sermon, *A Model of Christian Charity*, 1630.

2 *The Bulletproof George Washington*, David Barton, Wallbuilder Press, 2002.

3 http://nobullying.com/school-violence-statistics-is-it-happening-in-your-school/. Accessed September 19, 2015.

4 http://www.pewforum.org/2015/04/02/religious-projections-2010-2050/. Accessed August 24, 2015.

5 http://www.pewresearch.org/fact-tank/2015/05/15/compared-with-other-christian-groups-evangelicals-dropoff-is-less-steep//. Accessed October 19, 2015.

6 http://firstread.nbcnews.com/_news/2012/11/16/15219396-no-its-not-christians-fault-obama-won?lite. Accessed October 19, 2015.

7 http://www.history.com/news/10-things-you-may-not-know-about-the-war-of-1812. Accessed July 12, 2015.

8 Local meteorologists at the time recorded this conversation in their book, *Washington Weather*.

9 Charles Ryrie, *Ryrie Study Bible*, Moody Publishers, 1994.

10 Billy Graham, *My Heart Aches for America*, July 19, 2012, Billy Graham Evangelistic Association, http://billygraham.org/story/billy-graham-my-heart-aches-for-america/. Accessed September 27, 2015.

11 http://www.nytimes.com/2005/04/19/health/divorce-rate-its-not-as-high-as-you-think.html. Accessed September 21, 2015.

12 Letter written to the Officers of the First Brigade of the Third Division of the Militia of Massachusetts, October 11, 1798.

13 Letter to a friend, dated April 27, 1837, published in *The Historical Magazine* (July 1860), pp. 193-194.

14 George Barna, David Barton, *U-Turn: Restoring America to the Strength of Its Roots*, Frontline, 2014.

15 Ibid, citing William DeLoss Love, *The Fast and Thanksgiving Days of New England*, 1895, p. 464.

16 J. Edwin Orr, *Light of the Nations*, pp103-105

17 C.S. Lewis Institute archives, *Revival Born in a Prayer Meeting*, 2004.

18 From William J. Johnson, *George Washington, The Christian*, New York: The Abingdon Press, 1919.

19 William W. Woodward, *George Washington, The Image and the Man*, Reprint Services Corp, p. 142.

20 *The Writings of George Washington*, Washington, D.C. Government Printing, Vol. 15, p. 55.

21 Paul Vitz, *Religion and Traditional Values in Public School Textbooks*, excerpted from *National Affairs*, Issue 84, 1986.

22 Kenneth C. Davis, *Don't Know Much About History*, Harper Paperbacks, 2012.

23 Ibid.

Made in the USA
Columbia, SC
18 June 2019